D0349851

Confessions
of a
Horseshoer

Confessions

of a

Horseshoer

by
Ron Tatum

Number 8 in the Western Life Series
University of North Texas Press
Denton, Texas

10 9 8 7 6 5 4 3 2 1

Permissions:
University of North Texas Press
1155 Union Circle #311336
Denton, TX 76203-5017

The paper used in this book meets the minimum requirements of the
American National Standard for Permanence of Paper for Printed Library
Materials, z39.48.1984. Binding materials have been chosen for durability.

Library of Congress Cataloging-in-Publication Data
4871 2482 4/12
Tatum, Ron, 1955–
Confessions of a horseshoer / by Ron Tatum. — 1st ed.
p. cm. — (Number 8 in the Western life series)
ISBN 978-1-57441-453-0 (cloth : alk. paper)
ISBN 978-1-57441-461-5 (ebook)
1. Tatum, Ron, 1955– 2. Horseshoers—Oregon—Biography. 3. College
teachers—Oregon—Biography. 4. Horseshoers—Social life and customs.
5. Horseshoeing—California. 6. Horseshoeing—Oregon. 7. Fathers and sons.
I. Title. II. Series: Western life series ; no. 8.
SF907.T38   2012
682'.1—dc23
2012002038

Confessions of a Horseshoer is Number 8 in the Western Life Series.

Dedication

To my supportive, loving, always intriguing wife, Paulette.
(Her relentless pen made some sense
out of this whole thing.)

Sine Qua Non

Contents

Photos follow page 114

Preface

"It's not that horseshoeing is so hard,
it's just the dread of doing it."

Baxter Black

Some people might consider nailing pieces of metal on the feet of large, unpredictable animals a questionable way to make a living. I'll have to agree with those folks, and I often ask myself why I've been doing this for 37 years. I'm still working on an acceptable answer. Maybe writing this book will help me figure out why I've taken the paths I have. While I'm at it, I might also look at why I've decided to become a college professor as well as a horseshoer. I'm pretty sure my daddy had a lot to do with all of this. I'll look at that, too.

I like to shoe horses. I like to remember the experiences (most of them) over the years. I get to meet interesting horses, dogs, cats, and other animals. I get to meet interesting people, some of them interestingly unpleasant, who seem to enjoy talking to me, and for some reason often choose to share their lives and problems with me every eight weeks. I love the stories I hear from these people and their animals.

Maybe if I look closely at what I've been doing over these past years, I might even learn something new, myself. So this book is as much for me as it is for the reader.

I like to shoe horses and I like to write about shoeing horses, but talking about shoeing horses is not as enjoyable as it might sound. Horseshoers usually don't like to talk about their work. Like most horseshoers, I enjoy talking with other shoers about the vocation, but not with the general public. I get a bit cranky, probably because I often get the same response whenever someone asks what I do for a living. If I say I'm a horseshoer, they think I play horseshoes. If I say I put shoes on horses, they ask if they're like tennis shoes. If I say I'm a farrier, they just look at me funny. Recently, attempting a new approach, I told the nurse giving me a tetanus shot, "I shoe horses." She looked at me a moment and then said, waving her fingers, "You shoo horses? Do you make them go away using just your hand, or what?" I've run out of responses.

If they do understand my profession, they'll say something like: "Oh, you're a horseshoer! That's kind of a lost profession, isn't it?" No, there's more horses out there needing shoes than there were when they were our primary means of transportation. "Oh, that must be a really hard occupation!" Yes. "Oh, my grandfather was a horseshoer!" He was? "Oh, that must be a fascinating occupation!" Yes, it is. "Oh, do you enjoy your work?" Sometimes. And that's about as far as the conversation can go. I've said all I want about the occupation, and the person has probably lost interest, anyway. It's not a subject for small talk. When people at a party ask me what I do for a living, it's better if I make up something to avoid what invariably happens if I tell the truth. If I say I sell insurance or that I'm a dentist, I'm safe. No one wants to tell me their grandfather was a dentist, or that selling insurance must be a fascinating occupation. With that said, we can either part company or talk about something more interesting, like what *they* do for a living.

When people discover I'm a horseshoer, they invariably ask, "Do you have any horses?" I always answer, "No." I explain that I see enough horses every day, without having to look at one of my own. I like them, but I don't need one. Besides, if I had a horse or two, I'd probably never take care of their feet, and it's too much work to do for free. I'd have to pay some other shoer to do it. My best friend, Gary, is a good example of this. He's a horseshoer, but never took care of his wife's horse. She used to call me periodically to beg me to come shoe him. Every couple of months, she pleaded, "Ron, can you come out and shoe Hank? Gary said he would do it, but he never does!" I always charged her, too. They're divorced now.

Usually I don't shoe the horses of friends or anyone I know, because if they don't like my shoeing job, I might lose the friendship as well, or if the friendship goes awry, I lose a horse customer. What would happen if I lamed my wife's cousin's horse? Three people are going to be angry. And what would happen if my insurance broker thinks I did a bad job on his horse? We both would be angry, and there's an insurance policy at risk. This is the same reason I don't want to buy a used car from a friend. I often become friends with my customers, of course, but then when there's a problem with the shoeing, we usually can work it out. Gary, however, was an exception. If I did a poor job on his wife's horse, too bad.

Other people ask me, "Are your kids into horses?" Again, I answer, "No." I feel really lucky about this. They rode a lot of the horses back and forth between the stalls and the rack where I worked on them. That seemed to satisfy all four of my kids. I think they worried that if they showed an interest in horses, I would make them come shoeing with me every day. I supported their lack of interest. I avoided the expense and hassle of getting them involved with horses, and I didn't have to worry they would be hurt. I've seen too many horse disasters with people. My kids are all grown up now, and healthy. They still aren't interested in horses.

I'm not sure what got me interested in horses in the first place. It might have been Tom Mix, Roy Rogers, and Gene Autry, my heroes. I had a little cowboy bunkhouse bedroom out in the country near Tacoma, Washington, when I was three years old. Daddy was the caretaker of the grange and we lived in a little house on 2000 wooded acres. I had all the proper ropes, guns, hat, and chaps. I had horse posters on my wall and a large collection of toy cows. I always wore my cowboy hat in the house. After a huge battle with my mom and dad, I was finally persuaded to take it off at the table. It was that or no dinner. But out of the house, no one dared mess with me. I wandered around the fields and woods to look for cattle and the few horses on the property, and I always had my rope ready to catch one of them. It was quite an adventure to work my way through the woods along the narrow and winding paths through the trees, expecting at every turn to stumble onto a horse or cow. I never did find any, but I found fresh droppings. I had to be satisfied with that.

The next horse experience I remember was when I was five years old and my dad and snotty little sister and I went to Grangeville, Idaho, where Daddy, who was a competent athlete in all sports, conducted a summer swim clinic. I met the love of my life in that town, an older woman, but perfect for me all the same. She was probably a seventh grader. She had a horse and she loved me so much she let me ride it whenever I wanted. She even lent me her spurs. It was a wonderful summer for me, riding around town by myself, until fate struck a hard blow. I returned from a ride one day and after putting up the horse, I walked into the large tack room to find the love of my life in deep conversation with a boy her own age. I was crushed. I tore off her borrowed spurs, slung them across the cement floor in her general direction, and broken-hearted, but with head held high, I walked out of her life forever.

The rest of my childhood had only the occasional horse in it, like when as young boys we would climb into someone's pasture and ride their horses bareback until thrown off. I worked for a couple of summers as a camp counselor at a horse ranch where I received my first broken nose from Blaze, the fastest horse on the ranch, and the best stopper. From a full-out gallop in a reckless race around a regulation track with a bunch of teenagers on unpredictable horses, I pulled Blaze to a sudden stop. He threw back his head and smashed my nose, which was still moving forward. For some reason, probably youthful ignorance, I still liked horses. The fact that Daddy had been a real Texas cowboy in his youth probably had some influence. I think it still does.

Acknowledgments

My four wonderful children have greatly contributed to this book and to my life by their unswerving allegiance to being themselves and loving me no matter how bad I got. No one could ask for more.

My good old horseshoeing buddy, Gary Belvin, kept me on track with his down-to-earth, commonsense response to life. I'll always be thankful for our friendship.

Matt Bokovoy was enormously helpful in the initial editing. I thank him for all his support.

And . . . I couldn't have gotten anywhere without the suggestions, editing, and encouragement of Ron Chrisman from UNT. I've even forgiven him for scaring hell out of me.

Reflections Before Charging Ahead

That sentence about my daddy's influence has got me to thinking. Maybe before I go any further, I should try to figure out exactly why I've taken the paths I have. What were the influences that drove me toward horses and hard physical work, while at the same time driving me toward a bunch of graduate degrees? I'm pretty sure my dad had a lot to say about all this, but his influence also had some subtle aspects to it.

He started me off doing pushups probably about the time I first opened my eyes. I could pound the stuffings out of all my little friends by the time I was six months old. No one messed with me!

When I got older, Daddy didn't push me into sports even though he had been a professional football player, a boxer, an Olympic-caliber track man, etc. He was the complete athlete and had no insecurities on that score. I felt an unspoken push toward sports, but he who always talked with a loud and dominating voice never got on my case if I didn't excel in a sport, or even if I dropped out of one in mid-season. He was always pleased with any athletic trophies or prizes I

1

won, but never showed any disappointment in me if I failed. In fact one time when I only got second in a company picnic contest where I usually won everything, he blamed himself. That was an unusual event where my dad had to lie down on his back in the center of a circle of kids and whirl a big hawser rope around in a circle about a foot off the ground. The rope was 20 feet long and it must have been an incredible feat for him to swing it around as each kid tried to jump the rope as it swung by. If the kid tripped, he or she was eliminated. It finally came down to just me and another kid, and neither of us seemed to be tiring. Daddy told me to take off my jacket, and as I was doing that, I tripped on the rope as it came around. Afterwards my dad said it was his fault for asking me to take off my jacket. I was surprised.

I used to wonder why Daddy was so casual about my playing sports, but now I think I know what was going on in his mind. A lot of pushy dads who yell at their kids for striking out in Little League and making errors in other youth sports are probably frustrated high school jocks and are trying to live vicariously through the athletic successes of their kids. These dads most likely were not great athletes in their youth, but they want their kids to be the champions they never were. It's the male ego again.

My dad, however, *was* a successful athlete. He was a totally fulfilled athlete, excelling in all kinds of sports: football, track, baseball, basketball, boxing, watersports, handball, skiing, whatever. He didn't need to have the son win any trophies for the father's ego. He was big, competent, confident, aggressive, athletic, and a friend to everyone . . . except me, I thought. He encouraged me to always be in good condition, but didn't have any investment in my winning sports medals.

One exception: He was proud when I won the 6- to 12-year-old swimming race at the age of five. (They lied about my age so I could enter.) The race was a 50-yard swim from a raft in a lake to the shore. There were 15 kids entered. I won by mostly swimming underwater, since I didn't really know how to swim on the surface. First prize was a restaurant meal and movie tickets for the family, a sheet of candy suckers, and my picture in the paper.

My mother told me the story of how I learned my underwater swimming technique. I was two years old. At the lake in Tacoma where my dad was the lifeguard, a big log extended from the shore out into the water. The kids all ran out on the log, jumped off, swam to shore, and did it over and over again. There was even a German Shepherd who sometimes took his turn. (He also took turns going up the ladder to the high dive and jumping off. He never took cuts.) One day my mother was inattentively watching me when she looked up and saw me run out on the log. She jumped up to rescue her baby boy, but hesitated for a moment to see what I would do. I jumped in and disappeared under water. She had just started forward when I reappeared, a little closer to the shore. Down I went once more, coming up again closer to shore. I made it to shore in about six tries, got up on the log, and did it all over again. I didn't know how to swim, but I knew how to push off the bottom and struggle along under the surface.

Daddy was a fulfilled athlete, but he was not a fulfilled scholar. He worshipped his next older brother who was not a jock; he was a college professor. So Daddy tried to push himself in the direction his revered brother had taken. After graduating from college in 1927 with a teaching degree, my dad taught and coached at the junior high level, but he had no confidence in his intellectual abilities. He tried to improve himself. He read books about how to be a public speaker, how to increase your vocabulary, and how to win arguments through the use of logic, but he was never comfortable in his own mind. So he pushed me in that direction. Like the frustrated high school athlete pushes his son to excel in sports, my dad, the frustrated scholar, pushed me to excel academically. (Ironically, the respected college professor brother died trying to be an athlete. At one of his college reunions, he entered a foot race and died of a heart attack on the field. He was 58.)

Daddy was always on my case to get A's, only A's. Never mind the sports. They won't help you in life. Good grades will! He pushed me to get better grades by telling me I was stupid. I guess his theory was that I would try extra hard to prove him wrong. But he said this so often, I began to believe it. I can understand now that he was pushing so hard because he probably thought *he* was "stupid." He had no confidence in his ability to read and understand good books, or to carry on any kind of an intellectual conversation, so he pushed me toward what he had failed to accomplish.

It worked, to some extent. I always got good grades, even if I had to cheat. In the second grade I was the only child at the end of the school year who hadn't missed a spelling word on our weekly tests. In one of the last tests, I finished quickly, and while waiting, glanced at the girl's paper on the desk in front of me. She had spelled a word differently. So I changed mine. She turned out to be wrong, and it was her fault that my perfect record was broken. I was outraged and told the teacher that I had correctly spelled it at first. I showed her my paper so she could see what I had originally written and she could see that I had been correct. She gave me credit. I'm not sure I understand that teacher's reasoning, but I'm still proud of my perfect second grade spelling record.

So I spent my early years trying to figure out what I needed to do to get my dad to love or at least accept me. Being good in sports didn't work. But neither did getting good grades, because he expected that. My mother was always warmly pleased and proud of my grades, but my dad just looked at my A report cards, nodded, and went on with whatever he was doing.

I got frustrated trying to please him. I knew, at least subconsciously, that he wanted me to be a tough guy. That's why I got all those exercises and boxing lessons. (Of course my mother wanted me to be a little gentleman. She was so proud of me when I addressed older people politely, and used good manners in public.) But I also knew he wanted me to be a scholar and the kind of person who didn't have to read a thirty-days-to-a-better-vocabulary book. The problem was I didn't feel like I was doing either one of these things good enough for his approval. Somewhere in all my youthful confusion, I must have tried to be as much like my dad as I could. Maybe that would work. He was a lefty. I tried to become a lefty, on and off, clear into my adult years. (I almost got it, even though I about cut my throat trying to shave left-handed. I still notice immediately a left-handed person, and I'm really pleased that two of my children are left-handed.) And he had been a Texas cowboy when he was younger, helping to work the cattle on the family's large ranch. His family were cattle and horse people all the way back to the Revolutionary War. He always said, "They were all horse thieves." I think he was joking. (My wife, an avid genealogist, has done an in-depth study of my family and has discovered that they were mostly horse and cattle people. "It's in the blood," she says. The first immigrant Tatum took up ranching/farming in Virginia in 1619. One Drake ancestor was in the Marine Corps during the Revolutionary War. A Hogan ancestor was a "Long Hunter" friend of Daniel Boone, and the first schoolteacher in Tennessee.)

Daddy had lots of stories about his early days, but he never encouraged me to get involved in that kind of life, either.

All of this collected in my growing mind. What was I to make of it? Where could I fit in?

As I look back on my life, I realize I tried to fit it all in, one way or another. I tried being a lefty; I tried all the sports, knowing he didn't really care (but maybe he did); I tried being the compleat scholar. I tried all of these things for Daddy.

What amazes me is that I'm still trying. I've studied at 13 colleges or universities. I've picked up three master's degrees. I took up surfing at age 45, and collegiate wrestling at 55. And at the age of 70 I finally got my Ph.D. (Now *that* should please him!)

Daddy taught first aid and water safety most of his life and when I was in the third grade I started going with him to his classes. This continued all the way into my high school years. He used me to demonstrate some things and every now and then he let me teach portions of a class. He once told me I was the best teacher he had ever seen. That was his first clear message. So of course I started teaching everything I could, sometimes without having learned the subject myself. I still teach, and coach, and profess. Fortunately I thoroughly enjoy teaching.

But, just to make sure I covered all bases, I forced myself to become a Marine Corps officer, a Presbyterian minister, a stock market representative, a juvenile probation officer, a ski instructor, a licensed family counselor, a drug/alcohol counselor, a college professor, and a horseshoer. Somewhere in these lifestyle occupations I must have hoped to please Daddy. I probably knew he wasn't impressed with my choosing to shoe horses, but I probably hoped that deep down he would approve. (I have to use words like "probably" and "maybe" because I don't really know.) Maybe I pleased him, maybe I didn't.

He's gone now and in some ways I look back and feel my life has been empty and meaningless. I'm sure this feeling comes from all those years of trying to please Daddy rather than myself. I've had a lot of what other people call success, and I have enjoyed most of what I've done, but I guess I'm still working on who I am and what I want to be.

The First Horse

I put a shoe on my first horse at horseshoeing school. We students were all excited to finally get out of the classroom and put our hands on a live horse. We were working in pairs, each person required to put on one front and one hind shoe. The horses came from local skinflints who were willing to sacrifice the feet of their horses to inexperienced horseshoeing students in order to save the cost of a shoeing. The school charged nothing for this service, and, as I recall, that was the right price for our work.

Nervous students were working on the horses who had arrived, but my partner and I still waited for ours. We wandered around criticizing everyone's work, occasionally joined others in trying to make the first cut on the mid-summer, stone-hard feet of these first clients. It was hot and discouraging. I wondered what had possessed me to get involved in this ridiculous way of life, and I hadn't even started yet. Heat, fear, frustration, and a sense of hopelessness all mixed together.

Finally, someone pointed at an approaching truck and horse trailer racing down the narrow dirt road, careening around curves, sending clouds of dust swirling across the fields. The driver skidded to a halt in front of us, leisurely climbed out and opened up the trailer. Out flew this sweating, wild-eyed, black, giant of a horse, in a state of panic. He was probably 17 hands high. Our horse. My palms are getting sweaty even as I write this some 37 years after the fact.

My partner and I gaped at this animal as he snorted and plunged against the rope that the owner eventually tied him with. Then we gaped at each other. The instructor was saying something about this being an interesting case. Yes.

I went first. I picked up a front foot and got thrown about six feet forward. I still can't figure out how he did that. And I can't figure out how I ever got a shoe on that foot, but I did. I remember nothing about it, except that it took me something like 2 ½ hours to get my two shoes on, and that he kicked me in the leg with his hind foot. My partner started on the other hind foot, but by the time he got to the front foot, the horse had had enough. He'd been standing there, a nervous wreck, for about four hours, and he was through with the whole business. As soon as anyone touched this last leg, he kicked out violently. By this time, all the other students had finished their horses, and having become sated with watching the violence, had gone home—probably to reconsider the direction their lives were taking. Remaining were my partner and I, the owner, and the two instructors who reluctantly concluded that we would all be there until the horse died if they waited for us to get a shoe on that last foot. So the instructors took over. Failing miserably to secure a hold on the leg, the head instructor, who consistently and tenaciously had advocated that the shoer should never get angry or strike a horse in any way, started to yell, curse, and kick the horse in the belly. Nothing worked. My partner and I, from ten feet away, were enormously but quietly amused. Eventually the two instructors tied the foot up off the ground, and while one instructor hung from the horse by a lip chain, a very painful control device, the other managed to get that last shoe on. The horse owner, having enjoyed the entire spectacle, contentedly drove off with his horse into the dark, leaving the four of us to stare after him, two of us doing our best to hide the smiles that would have endangered our lives had they been seen.

Starting Out

I remember clearly one of my first encounters with a customer's horses. Just out of horseshoeing school, I had been an "official" horseshoer for about a week. The only dirt on my leather chaps was from dragging them around on the ground at the horseshoeing school. Everyone did this. It's embarrassing when you're a brand-new horseshoer. Customers watch you with skepticism and suspicion. But it's even worse being a brand-new horseshoer with a spotless pair of chaps. On this first day, I was helping my new customer and his son round up six or seven horses for me to work with. It was a hot, dusty day in Northern California and the horses were racing in all directions around the corral. When they ran toward me, I took off for the fence. "Don't run!" shouts the owner. "They won't run into you. Just stand there and head them toward me."

The owner told me to stand still with my arms outstretched. His 17-year-old son was doing the same thing about eight feet away from me. Horses everywhere. I watched the son who seemed to know how to do this correctly. As I watched in frozen fascination, two horses ran out of a cloud of dust right over the top of the son, wheeled around, and looked in my direction. I left the playing field.

The son survived. He had two broken ribs, but he was OK. I'll never forget him lying there flat on his back, sunken down in the dirt, a bewildered look on his face, and his arms dutifully outstretched.

That was a good learning experience for me. I've never believed anything a horse owner has told me since.

What Do Horses in the Wild Do?

This is a question I get all the time. People want to know how horses who aren't privileged to have a visit by a horseshoer every eight weeks get along by themselves. I'll try to shed light on that question, although, as with most questions about horses, there's a variety of conflicting answers. An old cowboy pal once told me about what he called the "Golden Trim," where, he claimed, shortly after the birth of the foal in the wild the mother chews off the excess growth of the new baby's hoof to the exact proportions needed for that baby. From then on, he said, the baby's foot would remain perfectly balanced in angle and length. (I couldn't help but picture in my mind the baby extending its foot to be carefully examined and chewed to the exact angles by the mother who had learned this in some kind of instinctive equine birthing clinic . . .) Then, my friend said, the horse will run around on perfect feet that will never need any work until it is caught by a human and ruined by restricting the terrain available to the horse, and by putting iron shoes on its previously perfect feet.

Along with the "Golden Trim," the idea of unrestricted terrain is my friend's favorite theory. He claims that horses

13

running free, like the mustangs, will stay on hard terrain until their feet get tender, and then move to softer ground. When the feet get too long because of the softer ground, the horses will move back to harder terrain to wear the hooves down to the proper length. That's one theory. A different one, endorsed by another friend, is that wild horses develop a rock-hard foot that can withstand any kind of terrain. They can go anywhere and run on any kind of ground, and their feet are just fine. I blame these two theories on two of my friends. I'm staying out of it.

I do know, however, that once humans get their hands on a horse, it's a different ball game. The horses can't choose their terrain for self-care, if that's the theory you prefer, and putting shoes on just starts a cycle of repairing the damage we've created. All that horseshoers do, really, is try to keep repairing the damage that we cause by putting the shoes on in the first place. By this I mean we'll take a flawlessly balanced foot, nail a metal shoe on it, and watch the foot grow all out of proportion over the next eight weeks. When we come back, we pull the shoe off and try to trim the foot back to balance again. You might, for example, start out with the correct (for that horse) 53-degree angles on the front feet when you put the shoes on. Then the foot starts growing and when you get back to it in eight weeks the angle has mysteriously changed to 50 degrees, putting a strain on the tendons, and the left foot has grown faster than the right foot, so it's a quarter inch longer. I've had the experience of trimming a horse's feet to the correct length, and find in eight weeks that one toe is longer than the other. The owner complains. So I trim the foot to the correct length, carefully measure it, have the owner carefully measure it to see that it is correct, and write it all down. Eight weeks later, I'll pull off the shoes and let the owner measure them. Surprise! One is longer than the other. It usually takes doing this a couple of times, but eventually the owner can see that the horse is a bit out of the usual and that one foot does, in fact, grow faster than the other. If you've made a tiny little error in balancing the foot, you'll notice with horror that it has expanded to where even your dog can see the difference in eight weeks. Then you'll pull the shoes, correct all the glaring and non-glaring discrepancies, nail another shoe on, and wait hopefully to see what it looks like in eight more weeks.

This is not to say that a competent shoer can't adjust for these problems and keep the feet in good shape, but it is to say that we scramble to keep the feet in the kind of condition they would naturally be in if the horses were left to run wild.

Recalcitrant Horses

This is a big part of every horseshoer's life. A whole book could be written on this subject. When shoers get together, the main topic of conversation, after the usual bragging about their famous horse customers, quickly gets to recalcitrant horses. We talk about our worst cases, about worst cases we've heard about, and we listen carefully to each other's stories because some day we may have to shoe those same horses.

The attitudes of shoers are as diverse as are the stories. Some shoers relish working with these difficult horses, even specializing in them. I've never understood this completely. I think it must be an adrenaline addiction. I know it's a real high to put the last, completed foot on the ground and step back from a crazy horse, but I'm sure as hell not going to seek out that kind of high. I can get my adrenaline highs from driving in freeway traffic or raising kids or suggesting to my wife that she seems to be putting on weight. I don't need extra adrenaline.

Other shoers, like me, won't have anything to do with crazy horses, at least knowingly. But when you first start shoeing, if you want any customers at all, you have to take what you can get. That often means you get the horses other shoers refuse to work on. And the customer, of course, won't mention that little problem. If you ask them why they are changing shoers (a useless question), they'll probably say something unflattering about the last shoer. "He never showed up," "He mistreated my horse," "He lamed my horse," "He was always late," etc., etc., etc. A lot of shoers have had their reputations tarnished by customers lying about their wacky horses. I've even had my name smeared by a woman who, while trying to talk a new shoer into doing her horse, said all kinds of bad things about how I had treated her horse, and I'd never been near her or her horse. It turned out that she couldn't remember the name of the last shoer, but she had seen my name in the phone book under "Horseshoers."

When people call me, I always ask how the horse behaves during shoeing. But they'll lie about that, too: "Oh, he's fine to work with. That last shoer had a little trouble with him, but that was because the shoer was yelling at him." Sometimes, in your initial innocence, you may forget to ask the caller how the horse behaves, and he or she doesn't volunteer anything. Then when you get to the job, you see this wild-eyed, ears back, snorting catastrophe just waiting for you to start something. If the owner is just standing there, at a distance, with a mask-like calm over her face, I suggest putting your tools down, going over to the owner, and looking closely at her eyes. If the pupils are dilated, go back to your toolbox, load up your truck, and get the hell out of there. The horse is crazy. So is the owner. She, or he, just wants to see the action.

After awhile you get so you can tell what the horse is like just from the initial phone call. If you ask how the horse behaves and you get a cheery, "Oh, he's just a doll. No trouble at all," go ahead and do it. But if the answer is "Uhhhhh . . . ," hang up. You've got a dangerous horse and an unconsciously honest owner.

Assuming you made the big mistake of not checking the references of your potential customer, and you go out to shoe the horse, and you are standing there with some puny tool in your hand, looking at a demented animal who is not going to go quietly . . . what do you do? The correct answer is to leave, but for the sake of this discussion let's assume that the horse belongs to your brand-new girlfriend who just adores brave, manly horseshoers who are so masterful with animals, or, if you're married, that your wife just reminded you that yesterday was her birthday and you have no money for a present. You obviously need to choose between giving up your girlfriend or your wife, and risking your life. So you decide to shoe the horse. How will this be done? In the next section, I will describe some methods I and others have used. I recommend none of them.

Other Ways to Get the Job Done

There are hundreds of tricks shoers use to get a difficult job done. Some are pretty simple, like the time Gary my horseshoeing buddy and I shod a difficult horse by picking up two feet at the same time. On the count of three I picked up his left front and Gary picked up his right hind. That left the horse only two legs to stand on and he was so worried about falling over that he stood quietly and didn't cause us any more trouble. Not overly imaginative, but it worked. (We didn't get to do this sort of thing very often because our wives decided to put a stop to our working together. We would go out and share the work on all of Gary's horses one day, and another time we would do the same with my customers. What disturbed our wives was that we would be out all day and half the night, and come home with 75 cents' profit after hitting every coffee shop, restaurant, and tack shop in the area. It was a good thing neither of us drank or we would have come home with less than 75 cents apiece.)

One of my apprentices told me about a more colorful incident that she had observed. A ranch foreman had a horse who was so much trouble to shoe that he couldn't find anyone to do the job. The horse could have been tied up and thrown to the ground, which would have worked, but the owner didn't want the horse to be thrown for fear of breaking his neck. So, one day he nailed a $100 check to a post. The check would go to whoever could get shoes on this disastrous animal. At this time, a typical shoeing cost about $25. Two shoers took him up on his challenge. They haltered the horse and blindfolded him. They then led him to a washing stand used for show cattle, a little area like a shallow bathtub. It had cement flooring with slightly raised sides about three inches in height, and a drain at the bottom for the water to get out. The shoers tied the blindfolded horse to the crossbar and put a wet towel over the drain. Then they turned a hose on and began filling the basin where the horse was standing. The horse was not much bothered by the water, and remained quiet while it reached a depth of about three inches. The shoers prepared to go to work. Standing in the water, one man got ready to pick up the first foot, an action that normally would have launched the horse into a raving, lunging lunatic. The second man stood by the horse's head with the running hose. Just as the first shoer picked up the foot, the other shoer poured water on the horse's nose. The horse froze. As expected, he was convinced that he was up to his nose in water and probably fearful of stepping off into deep water. The first shoer went to work and whenever the horse made the slightest movement, the second shoer poured more water on the nose. They successfully finished the job and led the sweating, trembling, but completely shod animal back to his owner, took the check off the post and drove off.

A different sort of water story has nothing to do with shoeing horses, but is about a horse who would not quietly unload from a trailer. He was willing to climb into the trailer quite placidly and ride to his destination in the best of spirits, but when it came time to unload, he had only one exit strategy: he backed out in a full blasting panic. Nothing the owners could do ever worked to get him to change this behavior until one day an old cowboy observed the horse's plunge out of the trailer and mildly said to the owner, "I can cure him of that." Willing to risk anything, the owner put the horse back in the trailer and turned the whole thing over to the old cowboy who drove the horse to a nearby lake and backed the trailer down the boat ramp. When he opened the gate to let the horse out, he jumped backwards right into several feet of water. The cowboy loaded the horse up again, drove around for awhile, came back and repeated the boat ramp experience. The second time was all it took, and when the cowboy drove the horse back to the owner and opened the gate to release the horse, he very quietly and cautiously backed out with perfect decorum. I'd guess he never blasted out of a trailer again.

Another story I'm not sure I believe is about a short, stocky, powerful shoer who put the difficult horse's front feet on his shoulders and walked him around until he gave up, probably out of humiliation. That doesn't sound too plausible to me, but my friend swore he saw it happen.

There are also ways of gently getting the job done, of course. Some of the more well-known horse trainers like Buck Brannaman, the advisor to Robert Redford in the movie, *Horse Whisperer*, and Monty Roberts, who sweet-talked the Queen of England's horses, would probably be able to talk the horse into putting on his own shoes, but most shoers I know don't have the time to spend training a horse for shoeing. I took the time to work with difficult horses, initially, but that was because I had few customers and nothing else to do. Besides, I always needed the money.

In one particular case, around the time when I normally took about an hour to shoe a horse, I had a new customer who warned me that no one had ever been able to put shoes on that horse's hind feet. I had a cancellation for that afternoon and decided I would give it a try. I had no problem with the front feet. The horse was quite relaxed and pleasant. But when I tried to pick up a hind foot, the horse kicked out viciously. I spend an additional hour per hind foot, picking up the foot, putting it down, picking it up, putting it down, until the horse either began to trust that I wouldn't hurt him, or just got bored with it all, and gave up. It took me an extra two hours, but I was able to finish the job. The horse was actually a quite pleasant horse, but some mistreatment or other had triggered off his vicious response to having his hind legs picked up. This was a basically decent horse, and I decided to keep him as a customer. In the following months, the time it took to finish his hind feet slowly diminished until he eventually stood quietly for all four feet.

Quite often when a horse gives you trouble with his feet, it's because lifting the leg hurts him. If you can figure out what the problem is, you can usually get around it in some way. For example, I've had a lot of horses who behaved just fine on their front feet, like the one I've just described, but would kick at you when you got to their hind feet. The problem was often in the horse's stifle joint, or knee. If you lifted the hind leg of a stifled (stiff kneed) horse, it would hurt and the horse would try to get his leg back. I discovered if you kept that leg close to the ground, it wouldn't cause as much pain for the horse and you could put shoes on him. For awhile I think horse owners considered me to be a magical farrier because I easily shod horses no one else had been able to do without using extreme measures. The secret was in the owner's description of their horse. If they said he was a really good horse in all ways except that he didn't like his hind feet picked up, I would say, "Well, I'll come out and give it a try." Nine times out of ten it was a stifle problem and if I kept the leg close to the ground, I wouldn't have any trouble. Sometimes I even had to rest the foot on something like a small box. I have a 31-year-old horse I still shoe where I rest the hind feet on an old metal army ammo box. The box belongs to the owner, but it has become such an important tool that I bought one for three dollars at a garage sale so I would always have one with me.

An added dimension to this discussion is that I believe stifle problems appear in older horses who are light in color.

I can just hear the groans of the one or two vets who might read this book, but that's what I've experienced. If someone calls me to do their horse and they tell me the whole story about it being a nice gentle horse, except for the hind feet, I'll ask them, "Is your horse an older one, and light colored?" If the answer is yes, I'll go out with complete confidence. I'll keep the hind legs close to the ground and 95 percent of the time I'll get the job done without difficulty. The owners think I'm a wizard. I always tell them the secret, however. They need to know their horse might have a stifle problem. Stifle on an older horse is no mystery; the color thing is. Just because it's not scientific doesn't change my own experience. I'm going to stick to that.

I won't try, however, to defend my decision to never shoe a completely white horse. Superstition does play a part in most horseshoers' lives, and I will never shoe an all-white horse, no matter how gentle it is. I think I got this idea from a realistic bad dream I once had. Another superstition for me and a lot of other shoers is that nothing should be said about how good a horse is acting until you are completely finished with the shoeing and you and your tools are out of range of the horse. Chances are good that if someone does say something prematurely stupid like how good this normally troublesome horse is acting, there will be trouble. The shoer should never say anything like this, and shouldn't let the horse owner say it, either. I've gotten pretty good at stopping an owner in mid-sentence who starts to make some comment like, "He's really being good, isn't he?" or, "It doesn't look like he's giving you any trouble this time." Just don't say anything until it's all over.

A Wyoming Cowboy

Recalcitrant horses can be tricked, outsmarted, manhandled, pushed, and shoved, but there is another way: listening to them.

All horseshoers talk to horses, but few horseshoers listen to what the horses have to say in return. One of those who listens is a tough old cowboy named Larry Swingle. At the time I knew him, he had spent twenty years as a horseshoer, during which time he began to study horse musculature and everything else he could find out about horses. He was friends with the right people so he had access to the bodies of dead horses, which he cut open and studied as closely as a first-year medical student working on a cadaver. He learned just about all there was to know about horse anatomy . . . more than the average veterinarian learned in school. During this process, he discovered that he could also communicate with horses. He could understand them. Eventually, he possessed the extraordinary ability to recognize a horse's physical abnormalities, and the equally extraordinary ability to communicate directly with the horse. Over a period of one year, I was a personal witness to these abilities.

I first met Larry seven years into my career through one of my customers who owned a California lay-up stable for horses injured on the race track. I provided the corrective shoeing recommended by the vets in order to get the horses healthy enough to get back on the track. A lay-up stable is a kind of a sick ward for horses, a curious place. This particular barn was immense, with thirty stalls on each side and a huge arena-like structure in the middle with hard dirt flooring. The horses were not happy in this place. For one thing, they were away from all that was familiar to them, no familiar stable mates, no familiar trainers or stall muckers. Some of them were used to having a goat buddy in their stalls, but that wasn't allowed in this strange place. And they didn't even get the daily exercise they were used to. It must have been what a jogger would feel if he or she were suddenly deprived of the daily run and stuck in a room to recuperate for a few weeks with no friends or family.

There was also the pain. It's hard for us insensitive humans to recognize pain in stoic animals, but it had to be there. Some of these horses had broken bones, torn tendons, ripped muscles, all kinds of injuries, usually as a direct result of racing accidents.

As you might imagine, most of these horses had a poor attitude, all of which made working with them more difficult than it would have been under normal circumstances. There was an air of tension and fear in this barn that I could feel every time I walked in the door. Because of this and the constant whinnying and stamping of feet, I was hesitant and fearful about working with these high-strung animals, even though I had been shoeing for several years. I'm sure this just contributed further to the bad energy. Under these circumstances, you could get yourself kicked by a horse you had easily shod for years.

My customer had read something about Larry in a magazine and asked him to come look at a particular horse problem. Larry, at the time, was well known for his ability to work on a horse whom all other medical remedies had failed to help, and restore him to good health. He was rumored to tell potential customers that he would not look at their horse until the vets had given up on him. The problem that my customer's horse had was that he couldn't walk. He couldn't move his left hind leg. Several vets had tried everything, including putting on a cast, but the leg still would not work. Larry, challenged by the situation, flew out from Wyoming to take a look at the horse. As the story was told to me by my customer, Larry went in the stall to observe the horse. After a moment he ran his hand down the horse's neck on the lame side. He looked at the horse for a moment and then punched him with a hard blow in the lower part of the neck. The horse almost dropped to his knees. Larry then told the handler to trot the horse out of the stall. Everyone simply stared at Larry. Finally, my customer said, "Trot? He can't even walk!" Larry repeated his order. After a moment's hesitation, the handler gently pulled on the lead rope and the horse began to move. He then moved to a trot.

Larry explained to the crowd that as he had moved his hand down the side of the horse's neck, he had watched the rippling movement of the muscles down the length of the body. As he reached the spot on the neck where he was to strike his blow, he noticed a lump raised on the lame hip. This told him there was a blockage in the neck at the spot where his hand was. By punching that spot, he released the blockage in the hip that had prevented movement.

Following his explanation, there was a lengthy period of silence. Then one of the bystanders said, "That punch really hurt that horse." "I told him it would," said Larry. Everyone looked at Larry. He stammered something in an effort at distraction, but the comment could not be withdrawn, altered, or explained away. The truth was out of the bag: Larry could communicate with horses.

The horse was restored to normalcy and had no further problems with that leg.

I was first introduced to Larry when my customer asked him to evaluate some of his injured race track horses. Larry and I shook hands and Larry just looked at me for a long time, obviously sizing me up. He then began a conversation with an opening I was to hear many times over the next year: "You probably have forgotten more than I ever knew about horseshoeing, but what do you think is the problem here?" I had heard that one before, and knew I was being set up. Larry's piercing gaze with a hint of a twinkle, completely gave him away. I was not going to fall for that "I'm just an old Wyoming cowboy" routine. And I never did. I saw him work it successfully on some vets and a few other people, much to his great glee, but whenever he pulled it on me, I immediately pleaded ignorance. When he realized he wasn't going to sucker me into claiming knowledge where there was none, he always launched into a lengthy, complicated, and amazingly accurate analysis of the "problem." He was remarkable.

He got me pretty good one time, however. We were looking at one of the horses I shod on a regular basis, and he told me to pick up the left front foot and look at it. I bent over to pick it up, but it wouldn't come off the ground. The horse wouldn't lift it. I struggled and pulled, but the leg wouldn't move. "What's your problem, boy?" he asked. "Don't you know how to pick up a horse's foot?" He shoved me aside, reached down and picked up the foot. "Like that," he said. Embarrassed and angered, I grabbed the foot and almost lifted the entire front end of the horse off the ground. Nothing. Then I noticed that Larry had his thumb stuck in the chest of the horse. He laughed like a little kid. "Got you!" he said. He then explained that he had been pressing on a nerve that prevented the horse from lifting that leg. Very funny.

Larry looked like what you might think a Wyoming Cowboy would look like. He was tall, kind of rangy, and always wore a comfortably fitting pair of jeans, old beat-up boots, a snap button faded blue plaid cowboy shirt, and a cowboy hat that was more beat up than any I had ever seen. It was a sturdy old thing that looked like it hadn't been off his head for at least thirty years, even while he slept. He was a laconic kind of guy, but when he did talk it was like you should be taking notes. I don't remember any small talk coming out of Larry. If he didn't have anything to say, he would just stand there and look at you. I at first thought he did that just to make people nervous so they would start blurting out a bunch of nonsense and he could set them straight, but as I got to know him better I realized that was just his way. If you wanted to babble out a bunch of meaningless words, that was all right with him. He'd just watch you and listen and when you were through, something of value might come up. One time when I had bought him a lobster dinner to thank him for his help with a horse, he found a staple in his lobster. He called over the pony-tailed waiter and told him there was a staple in the lobster. The waiter looked at Larry and waited for Larry to say what he wanted done about it. Larry just looked at the waiter and said nothing. Here we go, I thought to myself. The waiter started jigging around, shifting from one foot to the other, finally looking away from Larry's piercing gray eyes. Then, as I predicted, he asked Larry what he wanted done about it. Larry said nothing. The waiter started babbling, returned to the kitchen for a replacement lobster and didn't charge us for that dinner. All this without Larry saying a word. He was that kind of guy.

One of the first stories Larry told me had to do with his ability to communicate with horses. A lot of people claim to be able to do this, but Larry had unusual ways of demonstrating this ability.

When he first became aware that he could understand and communicate with horses, he decided to look deeper into this phenomenon, and enrolled in a course designed to enhance the psychic ability to communicate with horses. At the end of the second day, the instructor advised him to drop out because Larry knew more than the instructor and would learn nothing in the class that he didn't already know. Larry dropped the class. A few weeks later, he received a telephone call from the promoter of an upcoming rodeo who had been told by the instructor that Larry could talk to and control horses using only the power of his mind. The rodeo guy asked Larry if he could perform some of this kind of thing at the rodeo that was to be held in three weeks. Larry, at this time, had enough confidence in himself to agree to the proposition, and showed up at the rodeo at the scheduled time. He was told that three "wild" horses would be released into the arena for him to work with. The horses had never had so much as a halter put on them, had never even had their feet trimmed.

Larry stood in the center of the arena and waited for the horses. Probably encouraged to enter with the help of an electric cattle prod, the horses charged into the arena, saw Larry and stopped in their tracks. Larry gathered his thoughts and began to make mental contact with the horses. (Larry never called his ability "psychic," or ESP, or anything other than merely "talking" to the horse.) He never explained to me how he actually managed it, but he got the horses' attention and their confidence. Without using words, he convinced them to follow him around the arena. He led them over to the stands where he opened a gate and began an effort to get them to follow him up the stairs and along the aisles where the audience was sitting. He got the first horse under control and up on the stairs, and then concentrated on the other two. The second horse had already started up the steps, but the last horse became anxious as it approached the stairs. Larry experienced some anxiety of his own as he tried to keep the first horse under control, while at the same time concentrating on the last two. If he concentrated on one horse, the other two began to get out of control. The situation had all the makings of a huge wreck right in the stands. He finally got all three under control, led them down the aisles and back into the arena, to less than thunderous applause. Most of the people in the audience probably thought the horses were trained to do that trick, but anyone familiar with horses could see the raw, nervous, and flighty nature of those three animals, and appreciate Larry's talent for what it was.

Larry never again tried that stunt, but his reputation took a giant leap forward. He got calls from people who had been present at that rodeo, and he was interviewed by magazines and newspapers.

Larry enjoyed confounding people whenever the opportunity arose. He particularly enjoyed going after people who considered themselves superior in their knowledge of horses. Especially veterinarians. If he could convince these kinds of supercilious people that he was just the old cowboy that he appeared to be, he would lead them right into a carefully laid trap. He would let them "instruct" him about some complicated medical procedure until they had completely exposed themselves. No going back. Then he would say something like, "Well, I kinda figured it was like this . . ." and launch into a professional explanation of the subject that would leave no room for doubt. He would never argue with anybody. When he was done talking, the subject was crystal clear, and there was nothing more that could be said about it. The damage was done. The deserving victim could do nothing but stand there, bleeding in full view of everyone. It was a mistake to try to lord it over Larry.

But, if a sincere, straight-talking person was willing to learn, they had the opportunity. He would tell them what he thought they needed to know. He wouldn't tell them a word more than he thought they needed, but he would answer their questions.

There was, however, a bit of the rascal in Larry. He charged $500 to look at your horse, whether he fixed it or not. That was a lot of money thirty years ago. It still is. His customers swore by him and said $500 was worth whatever he did. He could watch a horse walk and tell from the movement of the larger muscles exactly what was wrong. Most of the problems were nerve blockages of some kind and most of the cure took place in the neck. Horse owners are rightfully concerned about the neck of their horse, and Larry often told potential customers in advance that he would probably be making some adjustments in the neck.

I remember one particularly hot and dusty day at a ranch, flies swarming everywhere, when a fashionably dressed lady who was not sure she trusted Larry, was not sure she wanted to part with $500, and was definitely not sure she wanted anyone messing with her horse's neck, approached him. Larry did not like to work with people who did not trust him. He explained to the lady that he would most likely need to make adjustments in the neck. "One needs to approach neck problems cautiously," Larry told the woman, "and there's always the possibility that my adjustment may kill your horse. It is equally possible that I may completely restore him to health. Either way, I will expect $500." The lady was in a spot. The vets had given up on her horse, but she didn't want it dead, especially if she had to pay $500 for the privilege. Larry told her to think about it and let him know her decision. She stared after him as he sauntered off to fix several other horses at the ranch. She paced back and forth, something her horse couldn't do, and after about two hours, came slowly over to Larry and said, "I want you to do it." Larry said he would, and after sitting around, leaning against a tree, and chatting aimlessly with me for half an hour, something we had never done before, he said, "Let's take a look at that horse." He had already figured out what its problem was, so he just walked up to it and punched it in the neck a couple of times, and the horse was sound. It could walk and trot. He took the $500 check, said, "Thank you," and walked off. The lady stared after him until he disappeared around the barn.

Larry had the good sense not to waste time trying to teach me anything about "communicating" with horses, but he did try to teach me some tricks about shoeing. "It's all about getting a level foot," Larry explained, "and you can't get a level foot if you don't know how to hold it." Most shoers just pick up a foot and start working on it. Most of us, also, have had the experience of trimming a foot to what we think is level, and having another shoer or someone else look at it and declare it not level. Occasionally, the foot will look just fine as you work on it, but it's not straight when you put it on the ground. It depends on how the foot is held as it is worked on. It was not uncommon for me to trim a foot that I thought was level, only to have Larry show me where it was significantly off. He showed me how to get a horse to stand before lifting the leg, and how to move the leg so you could see the true level. This was very important to Larry. He said that a ¼-inch error in the trimming of the foot would affect six inches in the large muscles. He often demonstrated this by showing me a foot that was off level and then walking the horse so I could observe the muscle movement in, for example, the hips. I would see a lump appear in a muscle as the horse walked. Larry would then remove the high spot on the foot with one or two swipes of the rasp. He would then walk the horse out and the lump would be gone.

Larry was adamant about this level foot business. I lived in constant fear of getting a rasp broken over my head for erroneously declaring a foot level. And he constantly tested me. One example of this testing game happened when he had someone walk a horse around so I could see how the foot was not landing flat. "Look at how that foot is not hitting flat," he demanded. I couldn't see it. Disgusted, Larry kept the horse walking around, asking me if I could see it now. No, sorry, I don't see it. After about my fourth failure to see it, and just as I was about to declare, "Oh! I see it now!" he said, "I was just testing you. It's flat." God knows what he would have said if I had given in. After that, I was extra careful not to BS Larry in any way.

Larry's ability to see the connection between muscle mass and the shape of the foot was legendary. A shoer who had run into Larry at one time, told me of his experience. Larry had been watching the shoer work, and from about 15 feet away had made some comment about a foot not being level. The shoer challenged him. Larry said he could determine the shape of the foot by the appearance of the muscles in the shoulders and hips. He said he could tell what was needed even if the horse was standing in six inches of sawdust. The shoer took up the gauntlet. He stood the horse in the sawdust and asked Larry what needed correcting. Larry gave the shoer instructions on what was needed and the shoer went to work. When he had made the changes suggested by Larry, the shoer stepped back and awaited Larry's comments. "Everything is fine," Larry said, except the right hind foot is still high on the inside heel." The shoer became an instant believer. He had left the right hind foot as it was.

He had pretended to work on it, but to test Larry, had not changed anything.

Larry taught me a lot, but I was never really certain that I completely understood what I was doing. He always had a kind of magic about him that denied understanding. I'm not sure where he is now, even if he is still alive. He was trying to find someone to teach his skills to, a full-time student who could afford the time and the expenses, but I don't know if he ever found that person. Larry would probably be in his 90s, now.

Druids, Celts, and Blacksmiths

I've been a student and professor of Celtic culture and Welsh language and literature, even longer than I've been a horseshoer, and have always been interested in the status of the farrier/blacksmith in druidical societies in medieval times. Back then, one person did all the jobs we now associate with blacksmiths, farriers, and horseshoers. Today, a blacksmith primarily works with metal, and a farrier primarily works with horses' feet. Horseshoer is just another more common name for farrier, although about half the time I tell someone I'm a horseshoer, they think I make my living playing horseshoes. "Farrier," from the Latin *ferrum* for "iron," isn't much better, since few people have any idea what the word means. It does raise a few eyebrows, however. In this section, I use the terms blacksmith, farrier, and horseshoer to mean the same person.

According to the sources I've studied, the blacksmith's position in the ancient tribes was equal to that of the doctor, just below that of the Druid, who was a rung below but occasionally equal to the king. The talents of the blacksmith in ancient Welsh and Irish societies were used to forge the

36

weapons, armor, and general armaments for defending a kingdom or attacking other kingdoms; additionally, the blacksmith was responsible for the horses and war chariots. But beyond these fundamentals, there remained a mystique about the blacksmith, the man who could manipulate and persuade the strongest of all materials, iron, into the service of the people.

The ancient Welsh and Irish developed a system of cultural beliefs around the blacksmith and his iron, some of which persist today. Consider the lucky horseshoe, a phenomenon as present in the twenty-first century as it was in medieval times. Popular belief has it that the shoe must be hung with the open side up so that the luck doesn't run out the bottom. I don't consider that view of a horseshoe as lucky at all. If I see a shoe in that position while it is attached to the horse it means I am standing behind the horse and in the process of being kicked. To explain: while working on a horse's foot, the horseshoer's view of the shoe is always with the closed end on top. This is because when you, as a shoer, pick up a front foot, for example, you stand facing the horse's tail and lift the foot in the direction of the tail. You then straddle the leg and hold the leg in place with knee pressure. When working with a hind foot, you again stand facing the tail, and put the leg across your inside thigh. In both these cases your view of the foot will have the closed end on top and the open end on the bottom. Hopefully the luck isn't running out. If you are looking at a shoe on the horse that has the open end on the top, it means the horse has kicked backwards . . . at you.

The luck associated with the horseshoe actually pertains to the magical and mystical qualities of the iron itself, and what the blacksmith is able to do with it. Most of the stories are about the blacksmith and the devil. In all these stories, the blacksmith outsmarts the devil and usually ends up causing the devil so much pain that he avoids any contact with blacksmiths from that time forward. Typical of these stories is one in which the devil, in disguise, comes to have the iron shoes on his cloven hoofs replaced, and the blacksmith, aware of the true identity of his customer, hammers the nails into the sensitive quick of the devil's feet. The devil limps off in pain, vowing to avoid all horseshoers from that time on. Out of this legend comes the horseshoer tradition of ending a work day by striking the anvil three times with the hammer to warn off the devil. I'm not entirely sure why I do this, but I find myself striking the anvil three times with my hammer at the end of each day. I always have.

In medieval Celtic communities blacksmiths were in the upper echelon of the social structure. So also, were the bards, the poets of the kings. If a person wanted to be a poet or a blacksmith, that person would have to be a freeman and undergo a strict training regimen under the tutelage of a journeyman blacksmith or poet. If, however, a slave or a non-free person were to secretly learn the skills of a blacksmith or poet, and could satisfactorily demonstrate them in the presence of experts, that person would automatically become a freeman. The catch was that if he failed to prove his expertise to the authorities, he would immediately be executed. The same fate was awarded to anyone caught in the process of learning these skills. I can understand an aspiring poet secretly learning the skills of a bard in a darkened room in the middle of the night, but where does an aspiring blacksmith go to secretly practice his skills? The sounds of a hammer striking an anvil would travel for miles in the woods. And in a society where horses are almost as important as people, where does he find the horses to practice on? It's hard enough for a new horseshoer in our times to find someone willing to risk their horse's feet on a beginner, but what must the attitude have been in the days when your horseshoer would be executed if caught shoeing your horse? I imagine the authorities would have had some unkind things to say to the customer, as well. Who knows? They may have executed the customer and his horse right along with the clandestine shoer. Perhaps the goal was worth the risk.

Becoming a horseshoer these days isn't as complicated as it was in medieval Celtic countries, except for dealing with friends, family, and wives who are horrified that you're giving up a "real" job for something that can get you killed and all dirty, and doesn't pay any money. So, with all that in mind I quit my job in the Stock Market and signed up for horse-shoeing school.

Horses and Marines

Another experience I had with horses before I really understood them, was on active duty in the Marine Corps. The Marines don't usually have a need for horses, but at one base I was the officer in charge of the stables at the Marine Corps mountain survival school, located high in the Sierra mountains of California. I was one of three officers and seven enlisted men who taught at the school. It was great duty. We taught skiing all winter long, often on skis for fifteen hours a day. And we taught rock climbing during the summer months. Our students were Marines from bases all over the world, many of whom had never seen snow, and some of them didn't know they had a fear of heights until they took our summer course. I was the only officer up to that time who completed a tour of duty at that base and never ended up in the hospital.

I was assigned to be in charge of the horses before I even knew what their purpose was. Some of my friends and I used to race them across the rocky meadows at an insane full gallop, but what the hell, we were Marines, weren't we? Besides, if we fell and injured ourselves we wouldn't have to risk our necks climbing around on those 1000-foot cliffs where we held our classes.

Toward the end of my first summer class I saw how the Marines were going to use the horses. They were the pack animals to carry climbing equipment, food, tents, and other necessities up the mountain where we held what we called a graduation climb at the end of each summer course. The exercise comprised three days of intense ice climbing, crevasse rescue practice, and finally, a full day's rope climb up the highest peaks.

We trailered the horses to the base of the mountain range and loaded the equipment on their backs. All the Marines carried large packs, curiously with very little in them other than personal clothing and equipment. I was puzzled by this. Why such large packs to carry so little?

Horses and Marines loaded, we slowly started up the five-mile vertical climb that would take us to our base camp. I was in good condition and thought this was a lark, light packs, beautiful scenery, other Marines to chat with, and a slow pace. What fun! After about two miles of pleasant meandering, the column stopped. I brought up the rear and had no idea what was going on. I jauntily walked up to the head of the column and saw a horse lying on the ground. "What happened," I asked. "Nothing," drawled the sergeant in charge. "This is where we unload the horses." Starting with the horse on the ground, the Marines unpacked the horses and loaded the gear into the formerly empty packs of the Marines who were then ordered up the trail, some fifty pounds heavier. No one seemed to notice my concern. "Why are we doing this?" I asked. "Is that horse injured, or what?" The sergeant looked at me for awhile before he spoke. "This is as far as the horses will go, *Lieutenant*. When old Toby lies down, that's it. There's no way you can get a single animal to take another step up that mountain. Since you're officer in charge of the stables, *Lieutenant*, you might be able to get them to move. You're welcome to try." I took my pack over to the horses, loaded it up, and started up the trail with the other Marines. With the extra fifty pounds on my back I wasn't as energetic as before. I looked back once and watched the sergeant lead the string of horses back down the trail. I'd swear they were all smiling.

The rest of the three days was routine except for the final graduation climb. Just prior to the climb the base had radioed me to return as soon as possible and report directly to the colonel. In trouble again. I was in charge of three students for the graduation ascent, and normally would have taken them up in two teams, each team, including myself, roped together. But since I was in a hurry, I had the three climbers rope together and I would do a free climb, unroped. I carried only my climbing tools and my 120-foot climbing rope. The cliff was new to me and about 800 feet straight up.

I led the climb and initially had no problems. The hand- and footholds were obvious and frequent. As we climbed higher, however, they began to be harder to find. Eventually they were almost non-existent. I wasn't worried about my three climbers below because they were roped together and were putting safety pitons in the rock and climbing one at a time. Two climbers were always in a stationary position to stop the third man from falling. I had no such protection and slowly began to worry. At one point it looked like I had reached an impasse. Nowhere to go. With each foot on a half-inch-wide ledge, I held on to another half-inch ledge with the fingers of one hand and groped for another handhold. Several of the rocks I reached for broke off and cascaded down on top of my three climbers. I could tell they doubted if there was actually a way out of there. They kept calling up, "You all right, Lieutenant?" I lied and shouted down that I was just looking for the best route.

What I thought was a good handhold broke off in my hand and I watched it fall some 800 feet to the rocks below. I decided I had had enough. I was ready to quit and just wanted to let go. I wanted someone else to take over for me and get me out of there. Maybe my dad, who was always ready to finish a job for me when I was a kid. Maybe God. Somebody. I wanted to give up and let go. The problem was that if I did, I would fall 800 feet to the rocks below. I hung there for awhile, looking down at the rocks, considering my options. It slowly became obvious that I had only one. Go on up. No one was going to save me. Only me.

The sun had gone down from our side of the mountain and it was getting cold. I put my fingers in my mouth to warm them, and I looked more closely at the rock for hand- and footholds. I continued to climb. After a few frightening mishaps, I reached what looked like a flat ledge. I reached for it, pulled myself up. I was on top, on a grassy patch of earth overlooking the entire Yosemite Valley enclosed in warm sunshine. I lay there for awhile basking in the warmth of the sunshine and the warmth of being alive, basking also in knowing that I alone had done it. The calls from my climbers hanging on in the cold dark below brought me out of my reverie. "Hey, Lieutenant! Are you up there? What's going on?" I told them to use their pitons and climb up carefully. They did, and about 45 minutes later the last climber reached the top. We were all pleased with ourselves and glad to be alive and on top.

I pointed out the best route for them to get off the mountain, chose a quicker route for myself, and off I went to face the irate colonel. I used my climbing rope to rappel down some of the easier cliffs, walked the dark trail expecting at every moment to stumble right into a bear, and found a staff car waiting for me in the parking lot. On the long drive back to the base I wondered what I was guilty of this time. As I recall, it was because I had told a superior officer what I thought of him.

Going It Alone

That experience on the mountain taught me a lesson that comes in handy as a horseshoer. Up there, hanging off the cliff, I was alone. No one was going to save me or get me out of that spot. Just me. Horseshoeing is a lot like that. I don't mean that shoeing horses is facing death every day, but it's an occupation that you do mostly by yourself. There is no one to bail you out when you get in trouble. If you run into a seemingly impossible task with no obvious way out, you need to find the way on your own. No one is going to rescue you.

Horseshoers choose to wear no one's uniform but their own, and those who survive the first year of horseshoeing (70 percent of first-year shoers drop out), prefer it that way. We're often called independent cusses.

In most occupations there is a continuous system of education, training, and what you might call "mentoring." A plumber or an electrician will undergo a period of training or education and then will usually go to work in a job where there is ongoing supervision. Once in the field, most workers will learn from their contacts with the boss and from other workers.

A teacher will graduate from a teachers' school and then go to work under the constant supervision/mentorship of a principal or a department chair.

Even doctors and lawyers will initially work under supervision and some sort of education and training.

In some of these jobs the person may eventually reach a level of competence where they can go into business or practice on their own, but they will probably maintain contact with others in their profession. They may also continue to grow and learn and gain support from societies, groups, and publications relevant to their occupation.

Horseshoers have it different. Most shoers will attend a horseshoeing school, and occasionally, but not often, go into a period of apprenticeship with an experienced shoer. There are a few horseshoeing publications to learn from, like the *American Farrier's Journal*, infrequent clinics to attend, and the occasional but rare contact with other shoers. In 37 years in the occupation, I've attended two horseshoer meetings and about four clinics. I've read a few horseshoer publications and a book or two. But that's about it. Like other shoers, I learned the business the hard way: under a horse. There was seldom anyone around to tell me how to do the difficult things, or how to deal with a troublesome horse. Over the years, of course, I have been around other shoers, and I talk about some of those experiences in this book, but as I write this it's been three years since I've even talked to another horseshoer besides the guy at the farrier's supply store. I've learned from experience, from my own mistakes. I can't think of too many other occupations that are so isolated. I'm not claiming to be special. This is the story of most horseshoers.

If you have horses, try to cut your horseshoer some slack. He or she is out there on their own, but if they survive the first year, they'll probably turn out OK. And, by the way, I say some discouraging words about horse owners in this book, but for every "unusual" owner, there are a couple dozen really fine people whom I can even call friends. They're just not as interesting to write about.

The Job

Sometimes I wonder about this job. I stand around in nasty stuff all day, wiping sweat and flies off my face, driving nails into the foot of an animal who could squash me if he hadn't been tricked into thinking that people were stronger and smarter than he was. It's a job that requires fast talking to get health insurance and a job that makes my wife ask me where I am bleeding when I get home. I think one reason I chose horseshoeing is that I had found little satisfaction in the other jobs I had been doing. I had been a juvenile probation officer, a minister, and an investment counselor, among other things, and at the end of a working day with those jobs, I never had a sense of accomplishment or completion. I had no way of measuring the value of my time. Did I help anyone, or not? I never knew for sure. I wanted something more concrete where I could look at my day and say, "This is what I did." (At 41, I was probably just having a mid-life crisis.) Looking for answers, I took a vocational preference test at a local college, but before I got the results back, I saw an ad in the paper for a local horseshoeing school. "That's it," I cried. "I'll become a horseshoer!" My wife at the time was not impressed. She threatened to take up belly dancing for revenge. I signed up for the school anyway.

The school was run by an amazing man who held a world championship horseshoeing record, and who had a Ph.D. and two master's degrees in animal sciences. He had us under his complete control from the first day. We were a motley crew with a few women, a mother and son team, a tired old man who actually sat under a pony to trim it (he dropped out), some long-haired types, a few macho boys, and an Irishman named Joe. Our collective group terror about what we were getting into initially led us into all kinds of disruptive behavior, but none of it made any difference to our instructor who straightened us out with no noticeable effort. He would make a comment like, "The coloreds should all be sent back to Africa where they came from," and the class would leap out of their seats in outrage. An hour later he would be supporting some extreme liberal position and talking about his sensitivity training group, and "Save the Whales," and "Stop the Nukes." Since we could never get him to come right out and argue with us, we finally just settled down in confusion and listened to the horse part. It wasn't until the end of the class that we discovered he was just pushing our various buttons all along. It had all been quite entertaining to him.

We were all excited during those first days of class, and couldn't wait to put on our new leather horseshoer's aprons (chaps) and try out our new box of tools that came with the class tuition. During breaks we cut weed stems with our new nippers, sharpened hoof knives that weren't dull, and some of the more eager students even tried on their aprons. "Look at me," one of the long-haired boys shouted, wearing his new chaps and waving a horseshoeing hammer around in the air, "I'm a horseshoer!" The rest of us, who of course were more sophisticated, waited until we were in the privacy of our own homes before we tried on our aprons and waved our new tools around in front of a mirror. "Look at me," I said in serious tones to my children that evening as I swaggered into the front room wearing my chaps and carrying a horseshoeing hammer. "This is what us horseshoers wear." My two lovely young children looked blankly at me for a moment, glanced at each other, and with the kind of unspoken communication kids possess, they forced a happy face and jumped up and down waving their arms. This came to an abrupt halt when their mother came into the room to see what the ruckus was about. The kids were familiar with their mother's attitude about Daddy becoming a horseshoer and clammed up immediately.

In the school we got a lot of classroom work and eventually a lot of practical field work where we practiced on real horses with real feet, most of them broken down in various stages of ruin. No one dropped out during the classroom sessions, but a few people left after they realized the futility of trying to nail pieces of metal to an animal's foot. The rest of us thought we had gotten pretty competent, however. We finally were able to shoe a horse in four or five hours. An experienced shoer wouldn't take more than an hour, but as long as there was not too much blood and the horse could walk away, we felt pretty cocky. Our graduation test was to shoe a horse in four hours with a reasonable degree of professionalism. Most of us thought "professionalism" meant the owner of the particular horse didn't tear off the shoes and throw them at us.

I was number one in the classroom portion and second or third in the practical work. I always felt I would have been number one in practical application, as well, if I hadn't been given all the flighty, gawd-awful animals. The instructor early on realized that Joe the Irishman and I had a quiet way with horses that resulted in our working together on all the bad ones. It would take us all day to shoe a recalcitrant horse, using our "quiet ways" of course, while the rest of the class could get two or more horses done in the same time. I don't remember exactly, but it may have been that our "quiet way" was just speechless terror.

Our class certainly had better working conditions than the group of devoted women horse lovers who years later enrolled in a course on how to trim their own horse's feet. This class was taught by a master farrier who had talked me into assisting him. It was a fairly simple class, and instead of live horses, we used freshly killed horse legs we got from the local slaughterhouse. They were full-sized legs with the feet attached. The feet came in all kinds of shapes and conditions, some with shoes on, some barefoot. We wrapped the bloody end of the leg in burlap so the students wouldn't get blood all over their designer jeans, and handed out the tools. Most of these students were true horse lovers and we almost lost the whole class when we brought these bloody, severed legs into the classroom. Several students got up to leave, but only two actually quit. The rest slowly adjusted, probably after dissociating the bloody stump in their lap from their own horse, and we got on with the class. After a couple of weeks the students had actually grown attached, so to speak, to their legs, even giving them names, like "old Paint," and "old Nelly." I would guess medical students who work on cadavers go through the same passage from abject horror to relaxed familiarity.

More on dead horse legs: One of my apprentices, Roger, worked as a night nurse in a hospital. In order to avoid laming some of my horse customers by letting Roger learn on them, I asked him to pick up some legs at the slaughterhouse to practice on. He got four good front leg specimens, two with shoes on, two without, the finer points of which made little difference to the terrified elderly day nurse who opened the hospital's refrigerator to discover four horse legs next to the flu serum. When Roger had trimmed and shaped those feet as far down as he could, I turned them over to my dogs. I knew they would eat the feet, but after seven months, they had eaten everything but the shoes Roger had nailed on. Everything. Leg bones and all. There was nothing left. They didn't bury them, either. I kept an eye on their culinary progress right up to the grisly end, and they ate every bite.

My first customer after I had finished horseshoeing school was a horse named Costalot. It took me four hours to shoe him. My young daughter and son who were excited to go with Dad on his first job lost their enthusiasm after about an hour and spent the rest of the time asking "Are you done yet?" After that they went shoeing with me only under duress. I had to resort to all kinds of trickery to get them to go with me. "We'll get ice cream cones after I'm done," never worked again after they had sat in the truck looking at each other for six hours. Promises of money and threats of military school had no effect whatever. Most of the time I never even got the bribe or threat out of my mouth, because they would run out of the house if I was even dressed like I was going shoeing. After awhile they got so they knew I was going shoeing almost before I did, and then they were nowhere to be found. My dog, Nicky, did the same thing in reverse. She knew when I was going out as soon as I thought about it, and she'd track me through the house, never letting me out of her sight, until it was time to go. If I was in the bathroom with the door shut, she'd be sitting right there when I came out, wagging her tail and looking expectantly. "Is it time to go yet?" I've come to the conclusion that ESP is part of the natural makeup of animals and children.

Not every trip was a disaster for the kids, however. My son, when he was twelve, and I had a great adventure at a rodeo in Willits, California, one weekend. I had come to shoe several horses and my son hoped to find some great-looking twelve-year-old girls. He came along quite willingly. He knew all about rodeo now, and never called those horses "Brucking Brontos," anymore. We had my best horseshoeing dog, Nicky, and dumb dog, Lucy (more on them later) with us. I shod the horses and we watched parts of the rodeo. Later in the day we noticed Lucy had somehow gotten untied and had disappeared. I wasn't worried too much, because I figured she would be back, and because I wouldn't have really cared if she didn't. After reflection, however, I realized this was my new girlfriend's dog, not mine, and that it was probably not a good idea to come home without her dog. (The wife previously mentioned had had her fill of being the wife of a horseshoer and had hit the trail.)

My son and I planned to spend only one day at the rodeo, but that all changed when Lucy still had not shown up by that evening. We decided to spend the night in the front seat of the truck and wait to see if Lucy would return. It was a particularly cold night and we had brought nothing that would keep us warm. Around two in the morning we walked into town to get something to eat and to get warm. We walked because we had to leave the truck where it was in case Lucy came back. Nicky was tied up in the back peacefully sleeping, probably dreaming about how pleasant life would be without Lucy. When we got to the all-night coffee shop and restaurant, it was full of rodeo people yelling and carrying on, and a guard at the door telling us we couldn't come in because there was no more room.

We were getting colder and hungrier by now. "Tell you what," I said to my innocent son. "Why don't you go around to the back and see if the cook might not let you in." (This wasn't just a shot in the dark. My son was good at getting things done. When he was eight years old, I watched him go into an ice cream store with no money, and walk out with a double decker ice cream cone.) About three minutes later, he was inside the restaurant telling everyone that his dad was outside and he was getting worried. They let me in and we got a good breakfast of eggs, bacon, pancakes, juice, and plenty of hot coffee.

We walked back to the truck and tried to sleep. Around four in the morning I was startled out of a light sleep by the sound of a dog barking in the distance. I got out to locate the sound. It was coming from a corporation yard about half a mile away. I walked over and found Lucy locked inside the cyclone fence. She wagged her tail rapidly and looked at me stupidly. There was no one around and the place was locked up tight. I debated leaving her there until morning, but her helpless (and stupid) look got to me. I climbed the fence, picked her up and carried her back over the fence. She ran off to the truck and leaped joyfully in the back, probably to the disappointment of Nicky.

The next day my son and I decided that, in spite of everything, we'd had a good time and we've talked about that adventure for years. We enjoyed the whole restaurant scene, particularly the young wannabee "cowboy" who was decked out in exactly the right kind of new hat, boots, and gear, except for his huge silver buckle that told the world he had won the barrel racing event at the Pendleton Roundup two years before. No one bothered to point out to him that barrel racing was a woman's event.

I've always enjoyed doing things with my kids, except for the time we were on vacation in Monterey, California, and my son and I were standing on a corner waiting for the light to change. A bus full of people pulled up to stop right in front of us. I had just said something insulting to my son, who was six at the time, and in front of an entire busload of faces looking our way, he swung a roundhouse left that caught me right in the nards. I was just able to see the hysterical faces of an entire bus as I doubled over in pain. And I couldn't even hit him in front of all those grinning spectators. "That was a good one, Son," I said, with a pained smile on my face for benefit of the audience.

The kids will go out shoeing with me now, but that's because they're grown up and want to make sure their old dad doesn't forget where he is and wander off into the woods somewhere.

That first day as a new horseshoer, I made $16. My wife at the time, the pessimist, pointed out to me that I had no other potential customers and that $16 wouldn't go very far. She also pointed out that, granted, I had that marvelous sense of accomplishment that I had been searching for and now had a real man's job where you showered after work instead of like those sissies who showered before work; and, granted, I was working outside, with my hands, and with animals as the vocational preference test had suggested. But, she explained, the idea of earning $16 for an entire day's work, if I could get it, was discouraging to her. I allowed that I could understand her position, but I persisted and somehow it all worked out.

I realized later that one of my wife's concerns was that she had heard most horse owners are women, and that for some reason, these women were attracted to male horseshoers. I wouldn't know about that. Maybe it's the smell. This reminds me of an incident with a woman and smell.

There is nothing quite like the smell of a horseshoer at the end of a hot day's work. After one particularly sweaty day, I took my checks into a local bank to deposit and the lady behind the counter pleasantly said, "I bet you have ferrets." I did have a ferret, and I knew exactly what she was talking about. Unless a ferret is de-scented the smell will knock birds out of the trees. But mine was de-scented. What the lady smelled was the horses. "It's not a ferret. It's horses," I said. This being a rural bank, the lady understood. We smiled at each other and parted company.

The Tools of the Trade

Horseshoeing tools haven't changed much since horses first started wearing shoes. If a Roman or Celtic horseshoer of old were to find himself in this century, he would have no problem shoeing a horse with the tools of today. I'll describe them.

The "shoeing box" holds most of the tools. It's usually made of wood, and has various sections for nails and tools of different sizes. The problem with a wooden box is that it breaks apart when it inevitably gets stepped on by the horse. Usually you can repair the box, but after my box had been stepped on and repaired four times, my seventh-grade son got disgusted and made me a new one in shop class. He added a clever invention: a three-foot cord attached to the box that would allow me to pull the box toward me if I got separated from it by the movement of the horse. I was really pleased with that addition, but it does have its drawbacks. For one, to a nervous horse, the cord looks just like a snake. A second problem can appear when you pull the box to you. Watching a box apparently moving by itself is unsettling to a lot of horses, especially if the box is moving toward them. I've learned to be cautious whenever I pull the box by the cord, but I'm quite pleased with my son's invention.

Some shoers, tired of repairing broken wooden boxes, buy aluminum ones. They aren't destroyed as easily as the wooden boxes, but they can be dangerous to the horse. A shoer friend of mine had a horse step down on a metal box and tear the tendons in his leg, a freak accident, but as I've mentioned earlier, if it can happen with a horse, it will.

You need to be cautious where you put the tool box, wooden or aluminum, while working on the horse. It needs to be close enough to reach, but it should never be in a position for you to trip over if the horse moves the wrong way . . . which he will do. I'll have to admit it's entertaining to those standing around when a horse pushes the shoer into the box and the shoer goes down into the dirt amidst a box of flying tools, nails, and curse words. I never see the humor in this when it happens to me, only when it happens to other shoers.

A powerful magnet is another important tool in the box. After the nail is driven into the hoof wall of the horse, the sharp end comes out the side of the wall, as it should, and the end of the nail is twisted off with the hammer and hopefully put in the box where the horse can't get injured by stepping on it. Sometimes, however, the nail end that is twisted off drops on the ground. If the ground surface is wood or asphalt or some solid substance, the nail ends are easily picked up. But if the ground is soft dirt, sawdust, or similar flooring, the nail ends sometimes disappear. This is where a strong magnet dragged through the dirt will locate the nails. I glue a smaller magnet on the end of my nailing hammer so if I drop a nail end, I just reverse the hammer, pick up the nail with the magnet, and put it in the tool box out of harm's way.

If the surface is solid, a lot of shoers just let the nail ends fall and sweep them up after the job is completed.

The magnet is also useful if (when) the horse knocks over the shoeing box in deep dirt. The magnet will locate nails, nail ends, and tools that might otherwise completely disappear in the dirt. I also have a larger magnet attached to my chaps where I put the nails. I like this better than putting nails in my mouth, as some shoers do. I haven't heard any stories about what happens when the shoer holds the nails in his or her mouth, but I bet there are some good ones.

More tools. A small but useful tool is the "hoof pick" that comes in all kinds of shapes and sizes, some even made in a forge by the shoer. They're needed to clean out the dirt and other nasty stuff that is usually jammed in the foot before you start working on it. Considerate customers will have the feet picked clean before the shoer arrives. This important little tool is the first to disappear in the dirt when the box is dumped over, so most shoers usually carry several. Some hoof picks have red handles so you can spot them easier. After the foot is cleaned out with the hoof pick, the shoer looks closely to be sure there isn't an infection, or a nail or rock embedded in the foot.

If the horse is wearing shoes, the next tools used should be a "clinch cutter" and hammer. With the cutter you break loose the nails that are clinched down on the outside of the hoof wall. This allows the shoe to be pulled off without damage to the hoof. I use the word "should" because some shoers go directly from the hoof pick to the "shoe puller," a plier-like tool that pulls the shoe off. The puller will take a shoe off whether the nail ends are loosened or not, but if the ends haven't been loosened, there's a good chance that part of the healthy hoof wall will break off with the shoe.

However it's done, once the shoe is off, the shoer will use the "hoof knife," a keenly sharpened tool for cutting away dead parts of the hoof in preparation for trimming the foot. (This knife will also cut away live parts of the shoer, if that person is not very careful.) There are right- and left-handed hoof knives. Most shoers have a little pocket on their chaps that holds the knife ready for easy access. This knife is very sharp and potentially dangerous, especially when pulled out of the pocket by the horse who then waves it around like the weapon it is. I've had several inquisitive and playful horses who thought waving a hoof knife around in the air was entertaining, especially when the shoer tries to get it back without getting a finger cut off. There are horses who enjoy this sort of thing.

After the foot is cleaned out with the hoof knife, the shoer uses the "nippers," a sharp, long-handled tool that works like a giant fingernail clipper. You need to be careful using this tool. A lot of inexperienced new shoers will breathe a sigh of relief when they haven't drawn blood with the hoof knife, only to be horrified when they cut too deep with the nippers and blood is everywhere. This is something to be avoided. It will hurt the horse and can cause serious lameness. (The problem here, of course, is that when you first start shoeing you don't know exactly how deep you can cut until you've had the edifying experience of actually locating the blood a few times.) The nippers are used to cut the excess growth down to a level where the shoe can be nailed on. The part of the foot you are cutting off is dead, like the end of a fingernail is dead. As with everything else in shoeing a horse, care must be taken at this stage because a miscalculation can take a big chunk out of the foot.

A large "rasp" that looks like a big metal file will be the next tool. Its purpose is to make sure each foot is level and has no rough or high spots. If not used carefully, the rasp will draw blood on the horse. And the shoer who carelessly picks up a rasp in the farriers' supply store will shed some of his own blood.

The rasp should never be used as a means of controlling horse behavior. At least that is the conclusion I've arrived at. The occasion for that lesson was a hot, dusty day when I was short of temper and trying to deal with a horse that was dancing around. He was a long-time customer and usually stopped his dancing if I told him to stop. On this particular day, I didn't have the patience to talk it over with him, so I smacked him in the neck with the flat side of the rasp. It wasn't a hard smack and it calmed him down. A few moments later, however, I noticed blood dripping down his neck. At first I couldn't think of any reason for this, until, Uh, oh, yeah . . . the rasp. Somehow the force had torn a tiny slit in his neck about two inches long. It wasn't the sharpness of the rasp that did the damage, but some kind of physics thing. I didn't think I had hit him hard, at all. I was puzzled and I felt bad.

My apprentice was with me that day, the apprentice who was also a nurse. He got a needle and some thread out of my first aid kit (sometimes shoers have to sew themselves up, too) and after medicating the wound, sewed the rip closed. It looked good to me. You could hardly see it. I called the owner that night and told him what had happened. He was a 6'4",

260-pound, bald-headed scary guy and I was glad he hadn't become upset. He was there eight weeks later when we went out to shoe that horse and its stable mate. He quietly watched us work, and when we were through, he said, "Thanks. Your bill for today's work is about what I paid the vet for coming out and repairing your sewing job. Now we're all even." My apprentice's feelings were hurt, but everything was OK with me. I had been afraid this guy was going to shoot me with the rifle he always carried in his truck and leave my body out there in the woods. I continued shoeing his horses in the future, as if nothing had ever happened, until I moved away. I never used a rasp to correct horse behavior again.

A typical rasp can have several lives. The first life for a brand new rasp is the finishing work on the hoof just before the shoe is nailed on. After a few weeks of that kind of use, the first stage rasp will begin to dull and then it's moved to the second stage after the shoe is firmly nailed on. The second stage rasp will smooth off the jagged nail edges and excess parts of the hoof wall. Since this step requires rasping against metal, you would never use a new rasp. The third stage comes after your rasp is too dull to do even this last job. Then it can be used as a "hot" rasp where it finishes off a heated shoe before the nailing. You will typically have three different rasps in rotation at all times.

Eventually, even the hot rasp becomes too dull for good work. But its life isn't necessarily over. Now it's ready to be used in woodwork where the degree of dullness is perfect. A sharp horseshoeing rasp will eat up wood, but a dull one works quite well. I give away a lot of these fourth stage rasps to friends and customers for their woodwork.

The rasp can also be used as a weapon. Holding onto its wooden handle, you can defend yourself against just about any kind of attack, except that of a ram. I really haven't had to use this step (except for that ram), but I'm prepared. The ram in question, here, wouldn't let me through the gate into the field where the horses grazed, so I gave him a little tap on the head with a rasp. He didn't move. I hit him harder. No response. I hit him some more, stopping short of breaking the rasp over his head, but he just stood there defiantly staring at me with his yellow eyes. He didn't even blink when I hit him. More worried about my rasp (they can cost up to $25) than his head, I just shoved him aside and went into the field. I guess I could have done that from the start, but like a lot of horseshoers I don't like to get stood down by an animal. This is an attitude that has got me into more trouble than just about anything else, and what is worse, the animals don't even care. Like they say, "Never wrestle with a pig. You'll get all muddy and the pig likes it."

Other less interesting aspects of the rasp: 1. Some shoers will heat up an old rasp in the forge and make a knife or some other tool or artistic creation out of it; 2. If you drop your rasp on the ground and the horse steps on it, it will break in half like it was made out of glass; 3. Some people like to stick them in their gardens with a little flag attached for ornamentation.

Assuming you haven't broken your rasp or done something stupid with it, and have successfully used it to make a nice level foot, the next step is to do the same on the other three feet. During this process you have to make sure the feet are balanced with each other in both toe length and angle, and that all other adjustments and corrections are made. (I'm not going to describe the myriad of corrective methods used for the distortions and therapeutic problems that all shoers have to face at one time or another.) A simple measurement error can easily lame a horse. Two tools are useful to prevent errors at this stage: a "hoof gauge" that measures angles, and a little metal ruler that is designed to fit against the front of the toe to accurately measure the length. You want to get angles and lengths right. It's discouraging to finish a shoeing job and then notice the feet are crooked when the horse walks off. After a few years of experience a good shoer can become accurate at making the right measurements without these two tools, so a lot of shoers just eyeball it. I still feel more comfortable using the tools.

When the feet are prepared, the shoes must be shaped to fit each foot. No two feet are ever alike, even on the same horse, so care must be taken to make each shoe fit each foot correctly. Just as a right-handed person might have a right hand larger than the left, so a horse that is, say, "left-handed" because it always starts off on that preferred foot, will have the front left foot larger and differently shaped from the right front foot. The tools needed for shaping the shoes are a heavy shaping hammer, an anvil probably weighing between 85 and 125 pounds, and, usually, a pair of tongs used to hold the shoe while shaping it. (Amazingly, at least to me, I've run into a lot of people who have no idea what an anvil is.) These tongs are essential if the shoer is using a forge to heat the shoe, but not always necessary if working with what is called "cold" shoes. (These shoes, bought in farrier supply stores, come in different sizes and are roughly shaped like a horse's foot.) I always use the tongs for either "hot" or "cold" shoeing, just because I've gotten used to them. The anvil usually sits on a special stand that must be unloaded close to the horse because you don't want to carry 125 unwieldy pounds for any distance. One of my customers had eight horses who were in stables located exactly 136 steep steps down from where I had to park my truck. I had to carry tools, horseshoes, anvil stand, and anvil down those 136 steps to shoe the horses. At the end of the job when I felt lucky to be able to carry my own body up those 136 steps to get in my truck and go home, I had to carry tools, used horseshoes, anvil stand, anvil, and my own body up those 136 steps. I often took the next day off.

Back to the shoe. Horseshoes come in a lot of shapes and sizes, from tiny little pony shoes to large draft-horse shoes. Some shoers use a forge to shape and finish the factory-made shoe; some just shape it cold. Other shoers start from scratch and make the shoes from steel bars by heating them in the forge, putting nail holes in them, and shaping them to the foot while they are hot. There are a lot of variations. (As I write all this, I keep thinking about the horseshoers who might read this book and periodically shout out that that's not how they do it, or that's not their experience of it, etc., etc. As I'm trying to suggest in this book, horseshoers are an independent crowd, and you can't always get agreement among them, even about the weather. You should hear what goes on at a farriers' meeting.) A propane or coal fire with an attached blower will usually power the forge. I have a coal forge made from an old water heater. It has a grate, a door, and a smoke stack that originally projected from the roof of my first horseshoeing truck. On rainy days, I would just put a shower cap over the top of the smoke stack to keep the rain from putting out my fire as I drove from one customer to another. The shower cap got a special mention one time in a San Francisco newspaper column. And the smoke drifting out of the forge as I drove down the road attracted special attention from the local cops a few times until they got used to it. I don't think they got used to the shower cap.

If you make your own shoes, you need a few more tools like fire tongs, buckets, coal rakes, and other tools for making nail holes and for cutting the hot metal. Most shoers, however, just buy pre-shaped shoes at the farriers' supply that will still need more shaping to fit the foot correctly. You need to be cautious when buying these ready-mades. American, Japanese, and some European shoes are generally reliable, but every now and then a new brand will come in from Korea, or Russia, or China, or some such place. They might be cheaper and look good, but they don't always work out. Russian shoes, for example, take a lot of hammering to get them to change shape when cold, and then, occasionally, they will restructure themselves right back into their original shape. Chinese and Korean shoes often have one side thicker than the other, a serious problem for balancing a horse.

To start out, you estimate the size shoe your horse will need, bring it to the foot, see what changes need to be made, and take it back to the anvil to make those changes with the big hammer. After you've done a few hundred horses, you can usually look at a foot on the ground, pick out the right shoe, and shape it correctly on the anvil even before you pick up the foot. Usually you will need a bit more adjustment, but an experienced eye can save a lot of time and effort. An inexperienced eye, on the other hand, can be a real pain. One day, while working on a horse in horseshoeing school, my partner and I had to make about two dozen trips from the foot to the anvil and back before getting the right shape on the first foot. At each and every one of these trips, the little twelve-year-old owner sitting jauntily on the fence asked, "Does it fit yet?" "Almost," we would reply. That was a particularly long day, but it gave us an idea of what to expect from horse owners, especially little twelve-year-old girl owners.

A crucial part in fitting the shoe is to make sure the nail holes in the shoes will direct the nails to the appropriate place on the foot. An error on one of those holes can allow a nail to be driven into the sensitive part of the foot, something to be avoided at all costs, or it can put a nail too close to the outside edge of the foot where it will rip through the hoof wall and have no holding power at best, and damage the hoof wall, at worst.

When all is ready, you nail on the shoe with the "nailing hammer," a spendy little tool, but usually the favorite of the shoer. These little hammers are perfectly balanced, except for the cheap one that came with the horseshoeing school's kit, and have all kinds of interesting shapes and designs for the discriminating shoer. The nails, themselves, are flat. The tip is beveled in one direction, the purpose being to drive the nail toward the outside of the hoof wall. The head of the nail has raised markings on one side that theoretically match the bevel so you can feel the head with your fingers in order to place the nail correctly, and hope that the nail head markings do, in fact, match the bevel. If they don't, and you don't look at the beveled end to make sure, you will drive the nail into the inner sensitive part of the foot. Experience will soon tell you by sound and feel where the nail is going and where it will come out. In 37 years of shoeing I have had only two nails where the beveled end did not match the markings on the head. In both these cases I had not checked the bevel, but the sound and feel of the nail going in warned me that the nail was turning in toward the foot, and I stopped hammering before any damage was done.

Something else to be avoided at the nailing stage is the situation where you have started a nail in a bad spot so that if driven in all the way it will go into the sensitive part of the foot . . . and to realize the danger at the very moment the horse jerks his foot away from you and stomps it on the ground driving the nail directly into the sensitive part of the foot that you were trying to avoid. This has happened to me, and it may well happen again. No matter how good you are or how much experience you have, you can't always avoid these kinds of accidents. Knowing this fact helps keep you humble and alert.

Assuming that you have avoided the hundreds of pitfalls awaiting the shoer, and you have the shoe nailed on, the next tool I use is a little block of steel called a "clinch block." The nails should come out of the sides of the hoof wall, usually three nails to a side, evenly spaced and about ½ to ¾ of an inch up the wall. The clinch block is placed under the nail end where it is held while the nail head is hammered, seating the nail securely. I then use my second stage rasp to smooth off the nail ends and make sure they are all the same length. They should look pretty and not have any sharp edges. Then what is called a "clincher" presses the nail ends firmly into the hoof wall. Not all shoers use this tool, some choosing to hold a clinch block on the nail head and use a hammer to pound the nail end flat against the wall.

When most shoers use the clinching tool, they will put the foot up on a "hoof stand" for easier access and to allow the use of both hands. Some of these stands are factory made, but mine is made from an old truck brake drum with a steel pipe about a foot long and an inch and a half wide welded vertically to the drum. The horse theoretically places his foot on top of the pipe and waits patiently while the clinching tool is applied and the second stage rasp finishes off the hoof. "Theoretically" is a significant word in horseshoeing. It means that there are a lot of things that should not happen, but do. Among a whole list of possibilities that can fly in the face of this "theoretical," in the case of the hoof stand, is the trauma experienced by the horse who, upon seeing this thing on the ground in front of him, puts his head down to smell it and inspect it more closely. The horse's eyes, located as they are on each side of his head, aren't well designed to see something like a narrow pipe pointing directly at them. If he has never seen a hoof stand before, a horse will often put his head down for a closer look and jam the pipe up a nostril. This often ends the usefulness of the hoof stand for that particular horse, who will in the future have nothing to do with a tool that so sneakily attacked him. If that happens, you have to pick up the foot and put it on your leg to finish it off. I like to use the hoof stand, so I carefully introduce it to new horses. It makes the job easier.

Once in a while, just for the acrobatic thrill, I'm sure, a horse will stand right up on the hoof stand with all his weight on a hind foot, balancing precariously in the air. One horse broke the weld on my stand by doing this.

Forges

When you work with a forge, whether propane or coal, you can experience complications that won't happen when you use cold shoes. One of these complications is the alarm that spreads when people see the large clouds of smoke pouring out when you do a poor job of lighting a coal forge. I no longer even look up when I hear fire engine sirens approaching my job site. I know some concerned citizen, thinking the woods were on fire, has reported smoke to the fire department. I've never gotten in trouble for this. Usually the firemen stand around and watch me work for awhile, and then with a warning to be careful, they drive off. On one occasion the firemen told me they had received 27 calls. That was a day when I was working in Northern California in the woods near a large civic center building. I'd had a hard time lighting the fire and the smoke was so thick I was about to call the fire department myself. After they had worked their way through the smoke, the firemen showed no particular concern. They watched and talked with me for awhile, gave me the standard warning about being careful, and drove off. The experience probably wasn't as exciting for them as a fire, but it must have been a bit out of the ordinary.

A forge can cause burns, too. But one thing horseshoers know is that if you burn your hand and immediately put it in the water bucket used for cooling off hot shoes, and leave it there until the pain goes away, the burn will be completely healed. I don't know why this works, but it always does. I've noticed a common reaction my body has if, for example, I accidentally touch something hot like the burner on my kitchen stove that I didn't think was on. The instant I touch it, I break out in a light sweat all over. Maybe that's the body's way of dipping the burned part in some kind of moisture. Who knows? A friend of mine was working with a red-hot shoe once, when it slipped from the tongs and ended up circled around his wrist. He shook his arm around for a moment, to no avail, and finally plunged his arm in the water bucket. He held it there for a couple of minutes, then pulled out his hand with attached shoe, removed the shoe and went back to work. He didn't even bother to glare at me for my obvious enjoyment of the whole scene. But that's what happens when horseshoers get together. There is hardly an accident of any kind that won't get the other horseshoers laughing at the unfortunate one. This guy had laughed at me often enough. It's worse if after some wreck, another horseshoer goes over to the victim and tries to look sincere and like he really cares about helping him, only to slip into sniggers or burst out laughing. I really hate that. I'd rather they just laughed out loud at me than pretend to be concerned while struggling to keep a straight face.

In Western movies you often see horseshoers working at a forge while shoeing a horse. My attention peaks when these scenes appear. I carefully look for authenticity. Does this actor know what he's doing? Is he using the proper tools, is he holding the horse's leg correctly? And my favorite scene test: Are the sounds of the hammer striking the shoe on the anvil the right sounds? Usually they are not. Most people know what a hammer striking an anvil sounds like. It has a distinctive ring to it. But a hammer striking a heated horse-shoe is a completely different sound. It doesn't ring; it just clunks. At home, when I see an actor playing the role of a horseshoer hitting a red-hot shoe with his hammer, and I hear the tell-tale ring of a hammer hitting cold steel, I always jump out of my chair shouting in outraged high dudgeon. At that point, my loving wife who has seen all this before, quietly leaves the room. When it's done right, however, like in the old movie *Bite the Bullet*, it's music to an old horseshoer's ears. My wife smiles.

(Another way I can spoil a movie for my wife is by pointing out that's a different horse from what the cowboy was riding just one second ago. Or by catching meaningless little errors like the closing scene in *Hidalgo* where the hero turns his horse out to run wild and free with the mustangs who have just been saved from slaughter, and you can see the horseshoes still on the feet of the released horse. Maybe the hero is going to bring the horse back after a little taste of freedom and remove the shoes. Maybe. But if he doesn't, those feet will be a disaster by the time the shoes fall off. My wife was interested the first few times I pointed out these sorts of inconsistencies in the movies, but now she just smiles that smile.)

You can cook food on forges, too. At least my female apprentice could. We were working on several horses on a cold day, and I had forgotten to bring my lunch sack that was probably sitting on the kitchen table at home with the house dog trying to stare it onto the floor where he could get at it. I told Ronnie, my apprentice, that I was starving. She laughed at me. While I was mulling that over, I smelled meat cooking somewhere. I thought it was coming from the customer's house until I went over to the forge and found a bunch of hot dogs wrapped in foil cooking on top of the coals. She had wrapped them in foil so they wouldn't have greasy coal smudge coated all over them. "I don't know the exact time necessary for cooking four hot dogs in foil on a coal forge," she said, "but these smell like they're done."

This was around the time when hurried and harried folks drove around with pork roasts, vegetables, and hamburgers wrapped in foil and tied to their car engines to be cooked while driving. There were recipes for how many miles and at what speed one would have to drive to cook a roast beef dinner with broccoli and béarnaise sauce to perfection. I think these people needed to re-examine their lives.

What the Well-Dressed Horseshoer Wears

Horseshoer's clothes are not particularly distinguished, but there are some peculiarities. Steel-toed boots are usually a good idea for protecting the farrier's foot from getting smashed, but there are always stories about some horseshoer or another getting his steel-toed boot stomped on by a heavy horse and having the steel plate trap his squashed toes in the boot. It would take a jaws-of-life (or jaws-of-foot) to get these squashed toes free from the boot. You would have to cut off the bottom of the boot to get them out. As gruesomely dangerous as this sounds, I've still always worn steel-toed boots. I haven't had my foot stepped on much, but I suspect I would if I even thought about going out in tennis shoes. And horseshoers being what they are, there's always someone who does wear tennis shoes. It's so they can get away fast, they'll say.

I never wear a ring while working with horses. I take off my wedding ring and put it somewhere safe in the truck, a long ways from the horse. I also put in the truck my wallet and everything else I don't want lost in the dirt. My fear about my ring, more like a nightmare, is that a horse will step on my hand and squash the ring flat with my finger inside it. I don't know anyone this has happened to, but it could happen.

Horseshoers almost always wear a hat with a brim, mostly to protect the eyes from a horse tail that's swishing at flies. Anyone who has ever gotten a tail whipped in their face will know what I'm talking about. When I first started shoeing horses, you could walk around a stable or a ranch and locate the shoer by the hat. It always had a brim and often was a baseball kind of cap, and no one else wore anything like it. Everyone wears a baseball cap now. I have one on, in my own home, as I write this, and if I'm not wearing a cowboy hat outside, I'm wearing a baseball cap. I've got nine different baseball caps and ten different cowboy hats, including hats for the grandchildren to wear when they visit.

Long-sleeved shirts are useful. In the summer they protect you from getting horse hair all over your sweaty arms, and in winter, they provide some warmth. For awhile, as a new shoer, I didn't wear a shirt at all in the summer. I got a good tan, but eventually became disgusted with the sticky horse hair all over my upper body. I gave up going shirtless one day when I had the front foot of my horse up on the hoof stand finishing it off, and the horse started licking my back. I couldn't get out of his reach and he would not be discouraged. I decided that day to go back to wearing shirts. The owners of that horse were amazed when they got there. They were new customers and since they were late arriving for the appointment, I had just gone in, got the horse out of his stall, and started working on him. They were baffled by their horse's behavior. "How'd you get him out of his stall?"

they asked. "He's really a spooky horse and he doesn't like strangers. And he's never very good with horseshoers, either." I had no answer for any of this. Maybe licking the sweat off my back was some kind of tranquilizer for him.

I knew a horseshoer who never wore a shirt in summer, a handsome, muscled up kind of guy that none of the other horseshoers liked. He always pointed out that the flies never landed on him because he was a vegetarian. "Flies don't bother vegetarians," he told all the meat-eaters who would listen. This guy was a showy kind of character, who always had a quick answer for everyone. The only time I saw him at a loss was after he told some old cowboy his theory that flies don't bother vegetarians, and the old cowboy smiled at him and said, "Horses are vegetarians, ain't they?"

Of course we wear heavier clothes in the winter, usually in layers because horseshoeing can be strenuous and, depending on the horse, you can easily work up a sweat. I've had occasions on a cold winter's day where I started a horse while wearing a T-shirt, long-sleeved shirt, sweater, vest, and lined jean jacket, only to remove these one at a time until I'm down to a sweaty T-shirt in 20-degree weather. The only gloves I've ever worn are wool and fingerless. I need to be able to feel what I'm working with. I can't imagine working with gloves, but I don't know what shoers in really cold climates do. I'm just glad I'm not there.

Most shoers wear jeans, lined ones in colder weather. I've yet to see a shoer working on a horse while wearing shorts, but I bet somewhere, sometime, that has happened or will happen. You just can never tell about horseshoers.

All the horseshoers I know wear chaps, a long, thick leather apron-like thing that protects the legs from nails, burns, horse bites, etc. These come in a lot of styles, but there are really only two kinds: suicide chaps, and all others. The "suicides" are those with a leather belt and buckle around the waist and hooks that tie the leg sections securely to the leg. The reason these are called "suicides" is because if your poorly tied horse freaks while, for example, a nail from his shoe is caught in your chaps, and the horse runs off . . . you will be going with him. By the time you can undo the belt around your waist and release the two hooks "securing" your legs, you and the horse could be half a mile down the road.

The other kind of chaps have a release system of some kind, like Velcro, that can be quickly released in an emergency so that the horse will be running down the road with just a pair of chaps attached to him instead of a horseshoer. The flapping chaps probably don't make the horse any more relaxed, but at least it's more enjoyable for the shoer to stand there and watch instead of being a participant. All this having been said, I still wear the "suicides," made specially for me by a friend. I just try not to do horses that might run off with me.

Weather

Shoeing horses is not a pleasant way to make a living, but when the weather is extreme, it is downright miserable. The extremes are heat, cold, and rain. It's best to stay home when these conditions are severe, but when you have no food in the house, you have to do what you have to do.

Heat, without question, is the most troublesome for me. I'll choose rain over heat, any day. In fact I will no longer shoe a horse on an extremely hot day unless there is a cool barn or some kind of shelter. I'm from the Northwest and we don't quite know what to do on hot days. We don't get a lot of them, so when it gets to be in the high eighties or nineties, everyone just stands around in confusion and complains. Air conditioners have arrived in most business offices and fast-food restaurants, but are seldom found in anyone's home. I only recently got a truck with an air conditioner.

One hot day in California during my first year of shoeing when I usually took two hours to shoe a horse under normal conditions, I took almost five hours to shoe one horse. I drank a lot of water, but the heat got to me. I'd work for awhile, get dizzy, and go into the hay room and lie down on a bale of hay until the dizziness went away. I turned a hose on my head and upper body every now and then, but that didn't

78

stop the dizziness. That horse stood out there the whole time in the blazing sun, mostly asleep, and didn't seem bothered at all by the heat. I probably suffered from heat stroke and didn't have the sense to recognize it. No one was around to point it out to me.

I apparently didn't learn anything from that experience because I continued to shoe horses in the direct sun for another three or four years, when finally, the lesson got through to me. The occasion was a 110-degree day in Northern California, on a Belgian draft horse ranch. The job was to simply pull the shoes off ten huge Belgians and trim their feet. No shoeing. The first horse should have convinced me to put up my tools and go home. The way it worked was that I would pick up a foot, cut the nail clinches, set the foot down, and rest, sweat breaking out. Then I would pick the foot up again, pull the shoe off, set the foot down, and rest. More sweat. Then I would pick up the foot, trim half of it, set it down and rest and sweat. . . . You can see the pattern. That first horse, who turned out to be the easiest one of the day, rocked back and forth the whole time I was working on it.

About five horses into this disaster, I took a break. I sat in the shade with my shirt off and listened to the old rancher tell me how this was nothing, and I should have been there in the old days when it was really hot. Then he began to bad-mouth another shoer, my best friend. I took a half-hour break, but even though I was in the shade, I couldn't stop the sweat from pouring out of me. At this stage of my life, I had no excess fat on me, and couldn't understand where the sweat was coming from. I started to worry, but had five horses to go, so I tried to ignore the problem and go back to work. The last five were worse than the first five and it took me longer to do them. I had to tie up the legs on two of them (see section on Different Kinds of Wrecks) in order to get them to stand. When I had finished, the owner tried to talk me down in price because of volume. No. I would not do that. He asked me to come back in a few weeks to put shoes back on the horses. No, again. Forget it. I thanked him for the lemonade and left, a wiser person. I took the next day off to recover, and never again shod another horse, big or small, on a hot day in direct sun.

Rain usually isn't much of a problem, at least here in Oregon, because everybody here is prepared for it. Horse owners have barns with shoeing stalls in them, or at least some kind of shelter. In Northern California, when I worked there, a lot of people had horses but no barns or stalls because the weather never was too extreme. The horses just stood out in the pastures and got wet when it rained. Every now and then, a neophyte overzealous horse owner would get upset when they saw their precious new horse standing out in the rain with no shelter anywhere. So they would build one. Then they didn't understand why the horse continued to stand out in a rainstorm when he had a nice, expensive new shelter to stand in. But that's how it is with horses. They do what they want and you'll never figure them out.

Other than dropping wet, slippery tools and getting soaked yourself, the biggest drawback to working in the rain is the mud. Dropped tools disappear in the mud, of course, but it's equally discouraging to prepare a neatly trimmed foot and have to set it down in the mud to go back to get more nails or a tool, or when the horse jerks his foot away and jams it down in the mud. It's like starting all over again when you pick the foot up. It will have an inch of gummy mud on the surface you had just so carefully prepared. A good bristle brush will help, but . . .

Working in the rain on a concrete surface reduces a lot of the aggravation, but the only good thing I can say about working in the rain is that it's better then working in the heat.

Shoeing a horse in snow and cold is uncomfortable, but preferable to heat and rain. Of course I don't really know what cold is, because, as I say, I live in the mild Northwest. I don't know how shoers can work in Montana or North Dakota and other parts of the country where the weather is extreme in the winter. For my case, the hardest part about working in the cold is frozen fingers. I like my fingerless gloves because I need to have direct finger contact with everything, but when the cold hits my fingers I could probably nail my thumb to the horse's foot and not notice. Sticking them in my mouth to warm them doesn't work, either.

Good lighting, although not exactly a weather issue, is important. This became apparent to me on a late afternoon in Sonoma County, California, as it was starting to get dark and I realized I hadn't allowed myself enough time to finish the shoeing. There were no lights in the horse's small shed, and I wasn't able to get my truck close enough for my headlights to help. The batteries on my flashlight had died. But there was a candle. I stuck the candle into the dirt directly under the horse's belly and fumbled through the rest of the job. I finished just as the candle burned out. The horse was quiet and didn't think there was anything unusual about getting shod in the dark. The real problem came after I had finished the shoeing. The space we were in was too crowded for a lady customer, a horse, a horseshoer, and Nicky, my dog. I hadn't noticed Nicky was in there. I thought she had gone to the truck. After the candle burned out, the whole group of us kept bumping into and stepping on each other in the complete dark. I couldn't find my tools, the lady kept stepping on my dog, and the horse started shifting around bumping into everyone else. I finally shouted, "Stop! Let's get organized here." I told the lady to find her horse's head and take him out . . . without stepping on my tool box. I got hold of Nicky, fumbled for the door, and took her down to the truck. I then went back, groped around until I located my tool box, and sat down to inventory what I could find by touch. Then I ran a complete mental inventory of what should have been in the box and came up a rasp and a hoof knife short. I sat there in the dirt for awhile, trying to conjure up enough night vision to see, but . . . nothing. I finally got in a corner and started to feel through the dirt in a pattern that I hoped would cover the whole area. Some time later I found the rasp and hoof knife, and my clinching tool that the mental inventory had missed. I called it quits, groped for the door, found my truck, looked around for the lady, who had gone home, and went home, myself, wondering what other tools I had left in the dark. If I lost anything else, at least I never missed it. I bought some extra batteries for my flashlight the next time they were on sale.

Injuries I Have Known

Injuries, and threats of injuries, are constant sources of fascination to a shoer. In the *old* days, horseshoers had a hard time getting life or medical insurance, so great was the risk of working with ill-mannered horses. Perhaps those old shoers had more macho pride or needed the money, but nowadays many horseshoers refuse to work with unmanageable horses. There are all kinds of restraining tricks and devices, but because these can prove dangerous to both the horse and the shoer, the best response is to tell the owner to get the horse some manners and then call. As one rusty old shoer told me, "I'm a horseshoer, not a horse trainer." If horseshoers practice this attitude enough, word will get out to horse owners that it is their responsibility to train the horse to stand quietly during a shoeing. That way no one gets hurt.

The best time to start the horse's training, of course, is shortly after birth. It's easy to pick up a foal's feet every day until it's no longer traumatic. I always suggest owners increase the noise and the fuss around the baby so it gets used to it. You can even tap the foot gently with a hammer—anything to get baby used to someone messing with the feet. If this is done with consistency, she should stand nicely for her first trim. After all this training, if she doesn't stand quietly, the owner might want to take a closer look at the shoer. Like children, horses sense fear, anger, and other emotions in people, and like children, they may try to get away from the source.

Once, a potential apprentice called me. He claimed to be good with animals. I was unable to take him, but wished him good luck. About two weeks later I was shoeing an old horse when a man in a brand-new shoer's apron came over to me and introduced himself as the one who had called. He had just started working with another shoer. I shook his hand and we talked for a minute. He looked over at my horse, always a nod or two away from being comatose, and under whom you could detonate a bomb without seriously disturbing his tranquility. The new shoer said, "Nice horse." He walked over to give it a pat on the head. The horse freaked. He jumped straight up in the air. Twisting and shaking his head like a newly caught mustang, he pulled back against the rope until he ripped the fence down. The apprentice ran like hell. When the guy was far enough away, the horse went back into his meditations. "Wow!" said the man who was good with animals, "That's some wild horse you've got there!" I glanced over at old Charlie, the ranch hand, who saw the entire scene. His face twitched in an effort to keep from bursting with laughter. "Yeah," I said. "He's a bad one. It's a tough life."

If the owner handles a baby with consistency, the results will usually be good. Unfortunately, many people don't stick with it. Like their decisions to spend ten minutes a day in exercise, or meditation, or reading something uplifting, they'll miss a day for some good reason, then another day or two.

Without ever knowing how it happened, it all comes to an end. That's how you create difficult horses.

Horse owners often think the shoer has enough experience to deal with the baby's first trim, and they cross their fingers and wait. This is not a good situation. Babies can be more dangerous than older horses. You can usually predict what an older horse will do. They shift their weight back and that could mean they're about to leap into the air; they lean slowly toward the foot you're working on, and that could mean they're about to drop to their knees. These indicators are fairly reliable. But you never know what a baby will do. They'll lean a little toward you, and fall on their back. They'll lift two feet off the ground at once. They'll softly nuzzle your shoulder and run right over the top of you. There is absolutely no guarantee that a given movement will be followed by anything you've experienced in your entire 25 or 30 years of trimming babies.

Enough on babies. If they're trained early and regularly, they should turn out just fine. But this section is supposed to be on injuries. Obviously a lot of them are caused by ill-mannered horses, but a lot of them just happen.

A new shoer must learn to get out of his or her own way. I've heard it said that if newlyweds put a bean in a jar every time they make love their first year, and take a bean out every time they make love in the years following, the jar will never be emptied. The same is pretty much true with horseshoeing accidents. I got most of my injuries in my first year of shoeing. My legs and hands are full of scars from horses who pulled their feet away with nails sticking out of the foot. My hands are scarred from cutting myself with the razor-sharp hoof knife. Very few accidents have happened since, because I've learned the signs that precede disaster.

A new apron isn't always a sign of a new horseshoer, but you can spot the beginner by the rips on the lower insides of his jeans and the Band-aids on his fingers. Let me explain.

If you drive the nail properly into the hoof, it comes out the side of the foot about ½ inch or more above where the shoe is attached. (Improperly done, the nail goes into the live part of the foot, an error immediately regretted by the horse, the shoer, and anyone within ten feet of the incident.) Exiting the hoof wall, the nail end usually sticks out at right angles. At this stage in the procedure, you would prefer that the horse not move. At this stage in the procedure, during your first year, the horse probably will move. Almost any kind of movement, from a violent jerk to a modest wiggle, can put ½ inch of nail into your leg or hand or whatever else is in the way. This is the kind of accident that can be anticipated and avoided with experience.

Nails coming out of the side of a horse's foot can be dangerous to the shoer and the horse. It can be downright horrifying to a sensitive animal-lover unfamiliar with the process. One gentle lady watched me shoe a little girl's pony, and became completely unglued when the nail came out the side of the foot. She shrieked incoherently and was on her way to call the Humane Society. The other little girls calmed her down and told her that everything was OK and that it didn't hurt the pony. She probably called the Humane Society anyway.

Most injuries involve blood. It will either be the blood of the horse or the blood of the shoer. On the very first day of

horseshoeing school, you learn what to do when you accidentally "quick" a horse (*i.e.*, make it bleed): cut your hand and tell
the owner that it's *your* blood. Owners do not like to see their
horse's blood. Jokes about the cut being a long way from the
heart will draw, at best, a baleful stare. If you can't fool them
into thinking it's your blood, at the moment of the atrocity
triumphantly declare, "There it is!" When they ask, "What?"
you say you found the "blood pocket." Now you can relieve
the pressure building up in the foot. If they don't believe you,
just leave and move to another town. They'll never forgive
you, and they'll bad-mouth you for the rest of their days.

If you lightly quick the horse when no one is around,
you'll probably get away with it. The horse's foot is remark-
ably adaptable and will most likely heal with no help from
anyone. Few horse owners and no vets will believe this. I
know all horseshoers will not only know it's true, but be mad
at me for saying it, but there it is.

Now that I've said all this damaging stuff, I must put in
a disclaimer. Not all horseshoers try to hide their errors. The
horseshoers I have known have been, almost without exception, honest and hard-working decent men and women with
a strong streak of independence and self-reliance made more
stable by some form of eccentricity. Many of them are well-
educated, with master's degrees, even Ph.D.'s. Most have an
innate intelligence and a strong sense of self-worth. The old
saying that a horseshoer must have short legs, size 44 coat,
size 4 hat, and be able to look through a keyhole with both
eyes at once is not true. At least not all of it. I have nothing
but respect for every shoer I have ever known, even the heavy
drinkers—with one exception.

In Northern California where I once worked, the local horseshoe supplier ran a store out of his home. He had a big, open barn behind his house where he kept the shoes, nails, and tools. Shoers came by at all hours of the day, picked out what they needed, and either went to the house to pay or simply wrote down a list of what they had taken to add to their bill. A wonderful and convenient honor system, very useful if you needed your supplies early in the morning or late at night, or if you just didn't have the money at the time. The system worked well for years, but it crashed down when one shoer and his wife were caught loading up boxes of shoes, nails, and tools, and driving off without recording them. The thief had been a respected shoer prior to this. He didn't know his entire act had been watched by the owner's mother who lived in a house on the hill above the supply barn. The trust was broken. Many of us were deeply affected and tried to apologize to the supplier for the behavior of this shoer. We were horribly chagrined. This was an entirely different kind of injury.

I'm sure there are other stories about dishonest shoers, but I haven't heard them. Horseshoers are decent people, even if some of them might try to hide blood they've drawn.

Another disclaimer: there are situations where horses left standing in their own urine and manure in a stall or in a field will develop an infection if you merely *think* about blood. If you quick a horse who's kept in this kind of place, you need to apply disinfectant and tell the owner to keep an eye out for infection. Call back later to make sure everything is all right.

More on injuries. A lot of shoers suffer from back problems, well, by spending so much time bent over. Once in awhile a shoer will pull a leg muscle. But most injuries come directly from the horse. I think every shoer has at least one horrific account of being flattened by a falling horse.

One of these typical stories happened to my friend Gary while he was working on a hind leg. This contortionist of a horse stepped on Gary's outside foot and slowly started to fall toward Gary, who couldn't get his foot loose. Pushing the horse back up was laughable, so he just braced himself for the inevitable crash. The horse settled down on his hind end, firmly squashing my friend, and then started to kick his legs frantically to get back up. Gary spat blood for several weeks and could hardly walk because of the beating his legs took from the horse's kicks. But he kept right on shoeing. Most shoers wouldn't think of going in for medical treatment.

You can avoid most injuries with a little caution, but it seems like the law of averages catches up with you sooner or later. You can't always watch fearfully for every potential disaster.

Some injuries are deserved. In a tale of instant payback, I had my nose broken for the fifth time by a horse who swung his head at me and flattened my nose with his jaw. He did that because I squeezed both his nostrils shut to cut off his air. This was my ridiculous attempt to show him who was boss, using a technique taught us by the quietly sadistic assistant horseshoeing instructor at the school.

A gentle old gelding once bit one of my apprentices on the head because he hurt the horse by holding the front foot too far away from the body. I had repeatedly warned him about the possible consequences of this position, but being a large man (too large for a shoer), he couldn't position himself comfortably under the horse. One of horseshoeing's maxims is that both the horse and the shoer must be comfortable. When he yelled, "Ow! This horse just bit me on the head!" I tried my best not to laugh.

Horses don't usually seek revenge against mistreatment, but ponies and mules might. If you successfully complete a shoeing job after a wild battle with a horse, you can walk away and everything is over. That is not true with the more intelligent pony. Many a greenhorn shoer, finishing the job and thinking the battle was over, has incautiously turned a back on an embittered pony only to receive a vicious kick or bite on his retreating figure. What intrigues me is that smaller animals seem to know they're going to get shoes, one way or another, so they give up the fight—and wait for one last shot at the shoer. Sort of a "Don't get mad, get even" attitude. The real victory for the pony in these cases is there is no recourse for the shoer. It's not only useless to hit the animal back, it looks pretty silly.

If a shoer hits a horse, it can easily lead to another injury: a broken hand from slugging the animal. I've seen two cases of this, and one case of a broken toe from kicking the critter in the belly.

Speaking of kicking. The most serious injury to the shoer comes from being kicked. There are hundreds of stories about being kicked, some tragic, some funny, but I will only describe the three times I've been kicked, all three occurring in my first year. I've already described the first kick from my first horse in horseshoeing school. The second time, a young stallion kicked me. This horse, according to the owner, was "pretty good to work with." At the time, I didn't know that meant the horse would let you catch him. He gave me some trouble while trimming his front feet, and I asked the owner if this was his first set of shoes. "Oh, no," he lied. "He's been shod before." There was no sign that he had ever had shoes on, no nail holes, no rasp marks. I doubt that he had ever been trimmed, let alone shod. In a fuzzy stupor, knowing I was in trouble, I began to struggle with the hind feet. I remember how time stood still as I watched both hind feet coming at my chest. Somehow he had swung me around to face his rear end. As the feet came toward me, I started running backward, also in slow motion. I got nowhere. Both hind feet caught me squarely in the chest. Fortunately, he didn't extend the kick, and it stopped right as it made contact. I wasn't hurt at all. I have no recollection of what happened after that, but I must have been foolish enough to finish the trimming part because I remember getting paid.

The third time, a horse kicked me with a hind foot right in the thigh. Two inches to the left and I would still be lying there. This kick happened because I was determined to catch this uncatchable animal. I had walked doggedly after him in a small corral until he finally got fed up and blasted me. With no owner around, I really went after him. Fearful of the stiffness that might set in, I decided to run it out. I took off my apron and ran after this horse, yelling, swearing, and waving my apron like a berserker. We must have run around that corral for twenty minutes. I never did catch him, but we both got a good workout and I wasn't stiff the next day.

The reason for all this foolishness arose because I fancied myself some kind of great horsecatcher in those days. I had had some success catching horses even the owners had trouble with, so I figured I had a magnificent and mystical talent, and I was going to be "Ron Tatum, the great horsecatcher." This delusion came about in part because I once caught an uncatchable horse in a huge pasture filled with horses. I had almost finished shoeing him when the ranch owner drove up and asked me what the hell I was doing with his horse. Wrong horse. I had caught and shod the wrong horse. "By the way," he said. "How'd you catch him? No one can catch him."

There are many odd little injuries, too numerous to mention. Some of them come from being stepped on. This is why some horseshoers wear steel-toed boots, as I've already mentioned, one way of guaranteeing you won't be stepped on at all—until the day you forget to wear them. Some shoers have taken on the bravado of wearing only tennis shoes. One of these, a friend of mine, said after the horse stepped on his toe it looked like a big sausage with all the stuffing coming out.

Every shoer has a favorite injury, many of them incredibly picturesque. Insignificant little accidents like the time a horse ran a nail into my wrist and the blood spouted up six inches, are nothing to some of these hardened injury mavens. But I do have one that is pretty hard to beat. Fellow shoers always snort derisively when I tell them I've suffered an accident that probably tops anything they've experienced, but they always look at me with new, if somewhat gleeful respect after I tell my story. It's about a pritchel.

A pritchel is an evenly shaped steel rod about eight inches long, wide as a thumb and roughly the shape of a piece of rebar or a railroad spike. It is pointed on one end and is used to punch nail holes in a piece of hot steel that you turn into a fitted horseshoe. These pritchels become dulled after extended use and need to be re-shaped, a process requiring that they be heated in the forge to a red heat and hammered into shape on the anvil. One day, while reshaping my pritchel, it slipped out of my grasp just as I hit it with the hammer. It spun upwards through the air and the sharp, hot end went up my right nostril. I could hear the hiss as it cauterized my nose. As fast as it happened, it was over, and I wasn't really hurt. However, I will not soon forget the 30 minutes of screaming, laughing, falling on the ground antics of two of my fellow-shoers, "friends," who witnessed the scene.

A lot of injuries to the shoer never occur, even though they should. I've done a lot of stupid things that should have inflicted injury on me, but thanks to the luck of the short and stocky, I've avoided some of them. Let me tell you about some times when I probably should have been hurt, but wasn't. All of them were my fault. They are stories about tying up an animal before working on it.

Where and how you tie up your animal matters. One time I tied the horse to a small hook on a vertical plank outside a barn. The horse pulled back, of course, and yanked the plank right off the barn. It was a one by six plank, about ten feet long, and it banged against the front legs of the horse as he ran backwards trying to get away from it. In a situation like this, it usually isn't helpful to try to talk the horse into calming down. I tried . . . and it didn't work, so I just had to stand there and watch him back up all over the barnyard, while this plank crashed against his legs. Finally, exhausted, he stopped and I released him. That ended the day's work. His legs needed a lot of vet attention. I was not invited back to finish the shoeing job, and I can't really blame the owner. I was the one who tied the horse up improperly. Also, in situations like this, no matter what the cause of an injury to a horse, if the horseshoer is anywhere around at the time, he or she will always be associated with the injury and not be welcomed back. This is bad when you have a full barn of horses as a regular customer and you lame the expensive horse belonging to the barn's trainer. There goes a large piece of your income. (I know what I am talking about here.)

On another memorable occasion, I tied the horse to a post on a customer's back porch. The horse jerked back, of course, and took the entire porch, steps and all, with him. The horse couldn't race around dragging a back porch with him, so he just stood there looking at it, and probably wondered why the house seemed to be following him. I have no idea why, but these nice customers blamed the porch instead of me, and kept me on as their regular shoer.

Another wreck, chosen out of many: I was asked to trim a large Hereford cow. The owner told me where to get the cow. Suspiciously, he didn't show up himself. I easily caught this huge gentle cow, tied it in a stall in the barn and started to trim the front feet. No problem. She was a nice old cow. Then I reached for a hind foot and ducked as it flew out in an incredibly fast and powerful kick that missed my head by only an inch or two. If forced to make a choice, I prefer to be kicked by a horse rather than a cow. A cow can really hurt you. I didn't try to pick up the foot after that, but tied one end of my lasso to the hind leg and threw the other end across a barn rafter overhead to set up a pulley to get the leg off the ground. As soon as I started to hoist up the leg, she kicked a couple of good ones, jerked the rafter from the overhead and ran out of the barn dragging the rafter behind her. I watched her run out into the field, stop, look around, and begin to graze. I looked at the section of the barn that had collapsed, got in my truck and went home. They could keep my rope. I never heard anything from the owner, and I never called.

Different Kinds of Wrecks

I've gone through a lot of halters and lead ropes over the years, especially early on in my career when I had to take any horse I could get, the bad and the good. I've been amazed at how a horse tied to a post can pull back hard enough to break a heavy halter or lead rope, although what breaks most of the time is the round metal ring on the halter that the lead rope is hooked to. The metal will usually break before the lead rope, or the halter itself. The trouble is if you break one of these metal connectors on either the lead rope or the halter, you usually have to just replace the whole thing.

In my third year of shoeing horses, I finally got fed up with all the horses who were breaking up my equipment, and went out and bought a monstrous, sturdy webbed halter that could have worked on a buffalo. It had a huge, round, heavy metal ring for hooking to the lead rope. I also bought an extra heavy lead rope with a snap link about the size of a small anchor. I had bought this rig especially for Cochise, a big old paint horse, who had broken up several of my halters and lead ropes. In my efforts to outsmart him, I had previously even tried tying an inner tube from a truck tire to the lead rope, a trick I had been assured would puzzle and confound the most determined pulling-back horse. (The simplest and most practical thing would have been to ask the owner to hold the horse for me, but in those stubborn days I did not think in either simple or practical terms.) When Cochise felt the give of the inner tube, he was momentarily surprised. He stopped pulling for a moment, thought about it some, pulled back some more, thought some more, and when he finally had reached the extreme end of the inner tube's give, he seemed to take a big breath and then, with a huge backward lunge, broke loose. Pieces of halter, lead rope, inner tube, and horse flew in all directions. Looking up at me from flat on his back, he seemed to be saying, "How did you like that?"

I enjoyed buying the big industrial-sized halter with its large iron ring. Now I've got him, I said to myself. He'll never break this one. For the life of me I can't remember how I ever got the job done before this. I most likely just turned him loose and he probably just stood there. I do not remember. I think the halter battle completely consumed me.

When I went out with this new gear the next time, I walked up to him in his stall and with a smirk on my face held the halter up for him to examine, placed this oversized contraption on his head and confidently led him out for the battle to begin. He was always gentle in every other way. He just didn't like to be tied. I tied him to the post and stood back, waiting. He looked over at me, looked up in the air for a moment, and let go with one of his best ever backward lunges. The metal ring snapped in half. I swear he laughed at me. I put shoes on him, probably while he was just standing there, took the disappointing halter to a welder and had an unbreakable steel ring welded on in place of the broken piece.

At the next shoeing, which had been constantly on my mind during the normal eight-week interval, he gave the thing a few tugs and gave up. I had won!

Now I felt bad. I felt like I had demoralized him, more interested in winning the battle than concerned about his feelings. I went up to him and spent about half an hour rubbing his neck and telling him what a fine horse he was and that I was sorry. After that we became the best of friends and never had any more trouble.

I think all shoers at one time or another decide to tie up a leg on a horse who is hard to control or that jumps around while they're trying to put shoes on him. There are all kinds of ways to tie up a leg, and some of the methods I've seen make the horse look like a Christmas gift, ropes going everywhere. I've seen some simple tie-up jobs on front legs that have one end of a rope around the neck and the other end holding the foot off the ground. And I've seen some that have the rope stretch from a fence in front of the horse back to take a few turns through the halter, around the neck a couple of times, and down to a bunch of loops around the front foot.

On the more complicated hind feet I've seen a rope tied to the tail, back around a tree to the hind leg so if the horse jerks his foot it pulls his tail. And I've seen some hind leg tie-ups that require about 50 feet of rope going all over the horse, and people hanging onto different parts of horse and rope. I've seen several of these methods tried on the same horse during the same shoeing attempt. Someone will say, "Hey, that's not working! I've got a better idea. Let's try this. . . ." The reason there might be a lot of people around offering suggestions is because anytime you've got a really difficult horse to shoe, there will mysteriously appear a whole crowd of people coming out of nowhere to watch and comment. God knows where all these people come from. It's like some spooky magnetic attraction drifts over the area, to draw people to where the action is. Each person will have a suggestion or a method that they know will work with this horse. When this happens to me, I'm always tempted to just hand them the tools and step back.

There is always danger in any kind of leg tie-up. The horse may still jump around on three legs and may fall and break a leg or even his neck. A friend of mine named Horseshoe Billy told me that he had once tied up a horse's front leg and the horse gave one more hop, fell, hit his head on the pavement and died. I can't imagine how I would explain this to an owner. But I know some shoers who would bill the dead horse's owner for the work that had been completed up to the time of death. If the horse couldn't be controlled except by tying up a leg, and he throws himself down, that's not the fault of the shoer, they will say. I guess.

Even worse than tying up a leg is actually throwing the recalcitrant horse down on the ground. This requires all kinds of feats of rope engineering, at least as many as there are for tying up a leg. If, finally, you get the horse to the ground without breaking his leg or his neck, you then find that you are the one in danger. The horse can kick and strike while lying on his side as well as he can standing up, maybe better because he can get all four legs into action at the same time. And by the time you've got all his legs securely tied up, you'll have trouble finding the foot in all the rope. Next you have to lie on your side or stand on your head to get the shoes on. People get comfortable doing things a certain way. When a new shoer starts out, everything is awkward and uncomfortable, but eventually it all becomes familiar and then any deviation is awkward. It's like asking a dentist to do a root canal while upside down. Eventually, I guess you could learn to perform root canals upside down, but it would take a lot of practice. That's what it's like to shoe a horse who is lying on its side with all its feet tied together. I don't enjoy a challenge as much as I used to, so I now leave those kinds of horses to other shoers. Throwing a horse has too many ways to harm a horse as well as shoer.

However, if an animal decides to put himself down on the ground, that's another issue. . . .

Recently I used a new method to trim Wilbur, a mammoth burro. He was a huge, fuzzy 33-year-old animal who had stopped shedding, even in the summer. He looked like a moth-eaten buffalo robe. Whenever he decided to lie down and rest, it was next to impossible to get him to his feet, especially for a hoof trimming. He liked it right where he was. On this day the owner spent several frustrating minutes trying to get Wilbur on his feet for the trimming, but Wilbur wasn't going to move. I asked the owner to hold Wilbur's head and I would try to trim him as he lay on the ground. It worked. Wilbur didn't move for the entire trimming. It was awkward, and I was fearful he would start kicking, but Wilbur didn't move. I had to look at him a couple of times to make sure he wasn't dead. I was very pleased to discover this method of trimming Wilbur because, as fine an old animal as he was, he still had a tendency to kick or to fall down in the middle of the trimming. I wish I had more customers like Wilbur.

Now cows, as I've already described, are something else. They do not like their hind legs picked up, and they're harder and more complicated to throw down, although they do have a better attitude about it. They don't seem to take it as personally as horses do. It's almost as if they'd like to help you if they knew what it was you wanted. My cow throwing experience is limited to two cows, but I remember them clearly. They both were young Herefords and they both were quite relaxed until I had hooked up all my ropes and started tugging to pull the cows to the ground. Their reactions weren't violent or aggressive, and, unlike a horse in the same circumstances, they weren't trying to kill me. They mostly were just trying to keep their balance, their equilibrium, to remain standing. As soon as I had them on the ground, it was like they understood. "Oh, yeah. I see what you were trying to do. OK." Then they just laid there quietly while I tied up their legs and trimmed their hooves. When I was through with the job, I untied the ropes and let them up. They stood there looking around for a moment and then began to graze right where they were standing. If they had been horses, they would have been in the next county by the time I picked up my ropes.

There is such a thing as a cow trimmer, a person who goes out to trim the hooves of cattle. These people have a cow-trimming table that turns on its side and you walk the cow up to it. They tie the animal to the table and mechanically rotate it so the cow ends up lying on its side with the feet sticking out in a position to be trimmed. This takes all the fun out of it, but I think I'd like to try one of these on some horses I know. Or some of the owners.

Not all injuries are self-inflicted, or at the hands of the horse, so to speak. Other creatures, like bees, can also contribute. One time, while I was driving to my first customer of the day, a bee flew in my truck and stung me on the left wrist. "I'll handle this problem," I confidently said to myself.

(Horseshoers, when tired of talking only to a horse or a dog, often carry on conversations with themselves.) "I will bring into play the old Marine Corps trick of doing strenuous pushups after getting shots." God knows where that half-baked theory came from, but the idea was that the exercise would get the blood moving and would carry away the stuff they injected in your arm, and then you wouldn't be stiff and sore the next day. It seemed to work in the Marine Corps, but it didn't work with a bee sting.

How I discovered it didn't work was because, instead of doing pushups, I decided to rush through two horseshoeings, working like a maniac, as fast as I could, with no breaks. I figured that would spread the poison and I wouldn't be sore the next day. But about the time I was finishing up the second horse, I could feel my left arm stiffening up. I tracked the pain moving up my arm, into my arm pit, across the back of my neck, into the other arm pit, and by the time I had finished the horse, the pain had gone from my left wrist all the way to my right wrist. Once firmly established, it began to seriously throb. I think it also must have affected my brain, because I went directly from the last horse to a job interview. I was applying for a part-time job as the director of a small hospital-based drug and alcohol program. My plan had been to get all cleaned up and presentable after the horses, but I showed up for the interview in my filthy, sweat-soaked work clothes (it had been 106 degrees outside), with swollen arms, and pupils that were probably the size of dimes. I have no idea what I said at that interview, if anything, but I didn't get the job.

Horseshoeing injuries aren't always bad, however. Sometimes they can work in your favor. You can blame the horses for injuries you've received somewhere else. This was quite useful to me when I took up wrestling, a dangerous, ridiculous, and senseless activity for someone my age, according to my wife at the time.

Growing up, I was a tough young kid, undefeated in neighborhood wrestling, and looked forward to being a wrestler when I went to high school. But during wrestling season I was on the swim team instead. I wasn't that good at swimming, but because of family loyalties and politics, the coach being a personal friend of my parents, I felt obligated to be a swimmer. After swimming workouts I used to go in the wrestling room where I could beat up some of the wrestlers.

In the middle of my rather prolonged mid-life crisis, I decided to officially start wrestling. I was 55 years old, but I was strong and fast, thanks in part to horseshoeing, and eager to make up for lost time. Stuffing my pride and self-esteem in my back pocket, I went to the wrestling workout of a local college and asked the coach if I could work out with them. He welcomed me, thinking I was an old experienced wrestler who could help him with the coaching. I said I really didn't know much about wrestling, but he thought I was just being modest. It became more clear to him when I started wrestling. I unorthodoxically grabbed my opponent and muscled him to the floor at which point the coach and I both realized I had just demonstrated the entire scope of my wrestling ability. He looked at me like an adolescent boy watching a hero topple off a pedestal. I grinned stupidly at him and repeated that I didn't know much about wrestling.

It was really hard to come back the next day, but I did. And the day after that. I kept coming to practice. I seldom

said anything, not wanting to compound my physical inepti-
tude with a demonstration of complete ignorance of what
wrestling was about. I worked hard at it, getting in wrestling
condition, learning some of the principles. Although getting
my butt kicked regularly, I began to improve. Soon I was
holding my own with the other wrestlers, and gaining their
respect because I worked as hard as any of them. I developed
enormous respect for wrestlers and, other than picking up
two cauliflower ears, thoroughly enjoyed being a part of it.

My wife at the time, on the other hand, thought I was
loony. "You're going to get killed," she regularly predicted.
"And when you do, don't expect any sympathy from me!"

And here is where I reconnect with my horse story. I
could blame the horses for all my wrestling black eyes, cuts,
and bruises. "Boy, I sure had a tough horse today," I would
grumble, watching her eyes for signs of disbelief. "He swung
his head around and smacked me right in the eye." Mostly
I got away with these fraudulent prevarications, but my two
cauliflower ears, swollen up like glazed donuts, couldn't be
explained away. I took the rap for them.

My best and most successful lie came after I had been
wrestling for about a year. I was working out with a high
school team when I ripped the biceps tendon off my left arm
during a wrestling practice. I remember hearing a distinct
pop as the tendon broke, and I also remember realizing how
serious it was and thanking God that I was going to be able
to blame this one on a horse.

My arm was all black and blue, but otherwise seemed all
right until one morning, a day or two later, I woke up with
the biceps muscle up around my shoulder. I immediately

went to my physical therapist who had been putting me back together since I started wrestling, but smiling sadly, he said this was a bit more serious and that I should probably see a doctor that very hour if I expected to use the arm again. They scheduled me for an operation almost immediately. The doctor said that too much time had elapsed and that even with a successful operation I would only have 30 percent of the use of my arm and wouldn't ever be able to fully extend it. Recovery, he said, would take an entire year.

I went into the operation with a lot of fear. The operation itself wasn't so frightening, but I was afraid I would die and the doctor, to whom I had admitted the truth about the accident, would let it slip to my wife who would then realize my entire life had been a lie and my children would have to face the future knowing their father was a prevaricator.

The operation was successful and I threw myself into the rehabilitation phase. My arm eventually healed completely. It took about three months and I got 100 percent of my strength back and can fully extend my arm. I still wrestle, mostly as a high school coach. My wife at the time still believes the injury was a horse accident. Of course that will end if she reads this.

During my recovery I was concerned that I would lose my horse customers. Then an acquaintance of mine told me he knew something about shoeing horses. Great! I jumped at the chance, figuring I could talk him through a shoeing or at least a trimming. So, with my arm in a cast, held up by a sling, I took him to my first post-operation customer. I chose a gentle horse we could do without the owner being present, and we pulled him out of his stall, in a huge, mostly empty, old barn.

Within minutes I realized my friend's experience had all come from reading a book. He had never previously laid a hand on a horse. Determined to do his best, he fought his nervousness and physical exhaustion and tried to trim a front foot under my careful tutelage. I had forgotten how hard it is for a neophyte to hold a horse's foot up long enough to do anything to it. A shoer in good condition can go through a full shoeing without taking a break, maybe even several shoeings, but a newcomer will need to set a foot down several times before finishing even that one foot. My new apprentice wasn't going to admit that he was either nervous or that his legs were beginning to fail him as he held the foot up, until he suddenly put the foot down, calmly looked at me and said, "Excuse me for a minute." He walked to the end of the barn, threw up his breakfast, and emptied his bowels in a vacant stall. He came back and said he felt better. I was stunned. Now what was I going to do about my customers? If this is what happened before he finished trimming the first foot, how was he going to get through seven or eight trimmings each day? I had to get myself back in the game. Those were nervous times for me. If my arm got pulled or jerked, the whole thing would have come apart, and the doctor had told me there would be no second chance.

I discovered that if I made good use of the sling, I could work on a foot, and that's what I did from then on. I continued to keep my friend with me, and he eventually became a good shoer himself. I of course told my wife that he was doing all the work, but since she washed my sling and my work clothes every day, I don't think she was fooled.

Exercise

After the operation on my arm, and a short period of physical therapy, I was briefly forced into a fitness center for what the doctor said was a "more thorough recovery."

I had never been able to see the value of a fitness center, maybe because I've always been in pretty good shape, thanks to my dad who had me doing 100 pushups a day and other exercises from the third grade on. My boyhood room was a huge unfinished attic and at one end he had made a gym for me. The floor was bare boards that didn't even reach the walls. There was a gap of about three inches where the floor tried to meet the wall, and if you ever dropped a toy down there, it was gone forever, into the bowels of the earth, I thought. Behind the darkened chimney in the corner was where the monsters lived. One did not even look in that direction come bedtime. The gym had weights, a wrestling mat, a huge body bag for punching, and a thick rope that rose to the unfinished rafters above the mat, crossed the entire room, and dropped down on the upper bunk where I slept in a tiny civilized section of the room. The bedroom part had a tiny rug, a tiny desk and chair, and my bunk bed. I was supposed to climb up the rope at the far end of the room, climb hand over hand to my upper bunk, and lower myself to bed at night. In the morning, I was to reverse the process, climb up from my bed, cross hand over hand to the other end, lower myself to the mat, go downstairs, eat breakfast, and go off to school, a splendid physical specimen of a third grader.

I didn't mind doing this too much because Daddy had me convinced there was some huge, albeit intangible reward for all of my efforts. I, however, altered the routine when I discovered that in the morning I could jump for the horizontal part of the rope instead of climbing up to it. I started doing this because the rope hurt my hands in the morning. One morning I jumped for the rope from my top bunk, missed, and fell flat on my face onto the floor. My dad heard the crash and ran up to see what had happened. He picked me up, carried me downstairs, and told me I didn't have to do that anymore. I loved him for that, and determined to stick with it from then on. I wasn't going to be no sissy.

In high school I was able to profit from the rope-climbing exercise when I set the school record for the rope climb. (Later in college I came within a fraction of a second of setting the U.S. college record for the 20-foot rope climb that at the time was a part of gymnastics.) When the high school track coach noticed that I had broken the school record, he knew he had the perfect man for the pole vault. He spent an entire afternoon with me, ignoring the rest of the track team, discussing the dynamics of pole vaulting, showing me movies of the sport, etc., etc. I never believed any of it. I would watch the movie where the pole vaulter was running with his pole toward the jump, and at each step I would say to myself, "He'll never make it." It looked physically impossible. I so convinced myself it couldn't be done that I was never able to vault more than a foot or two. I could jump higher than I could pole vault. The mind is a wonderful and frightening thing.

Back to my bedroom gymnasium. I boxed the bag, climbed the rope, lifted the weights, did my pushups, and boxed with my dad. Fighting with my dad was a real frustration. He boxed on his knees, but the gloves were so big I couldn't get past them to him. All I remember was a big mass of boxing gloves, his and mine, in my own face. He never really hit me, but I never got a good shot at him either. It was so frustrating that I usually ended up in tears. I would really have liked to have gotten one clear shot at him.

I guess he decided our sparring lessons weren't helping much, so one day he suggested I ask the toughest kid in my class to come home with me to box. I thought the idea was not just embarrassing, but stupid as well. But you didn't argue with my dad. So I approached Johnny West the next day and invited him to come to my house after school. "What for?" he asked. "Is it a party, or what?" I told him it was a surprise. All day he kept asking me what the surprise was, and I kept telling him he would find out when we got to my house. He was quite excited and I was feeling more stupid as the day dragged on. I knew if I told him the real reason, he would just tell me to forget it. After school we ran excitedly to my house, went upstairs to my little gym, where I got out the boxing gloves and said, "Here's the surprise. We're going to box." He just looked at me. No ice cream, no cake, no toys. Boxing. Great. We put on the gloves and jumped around trying to hit each other for about 45 seconds. The boxing gloves were bigger than we were and I don't think a single blow was landed. He finally stopped, took off the gloves and started playing with some of my toys. I just watched him for awhile. Then we ate some peanut butter sandwiches and went out to play catch. Neither of us ever mentioned the boxing match again.

Back to the fitness center. I stayed with my exercise recovery program for a few months and then abruptly dropped it. But life goes on. Now I'm in my late 70s and I'm once again in a fitness center because my life as a high school wrestling coach requires that I wreck myself on a regular basis by insisting on wrestling with younger people; and every now and then, I still get the snot knocked out of me by a horse. I go to the center to repair various body parts injured in the line of action. Not much has changed at the fitness center.

The fitness center. Quite an interesting culture. I sometimes become more absorbed in watching what is going on than in doing my own exercises. There appear to be a lot of unwritten rules in these places. One of them is that you don't make eye contact with anyone. The trainers never look at you, and neither do your fellow exercisers. It took me a while to figure this out, but I think I have it now. I think there are two reasons. One is that a person in the middle of some exercise is probably concentrating and should not be distracted by someone looking at them. I think that's probably the main reason the trainers don't make eye contact with anyone. They don't want to break up your concentration. They don't even make eye contact when you check in with your membership card. One time, however, there was an exception to this unwritten rule. The club's management obviously decided the staff should be more friendly to the patrons, so the staff must have been told to smile, look patrons in the eye when they come in, and, just like a Starbucks coffee server, ask them how their day is going. This caused a lot of strained facial muscles, but for two days there were smiling faces and direct eyeball-to-eyeball contacts with patrons. Then it all abruptly stopped. Maybe some of the patrons complained that it was getting entirely too personal.

Another reason for no eye contact, I think, is because what many people are doing is blatantly trying to make themselves look better. More muscles, better figure, pick up the chicks, attract the guys. How embarrassing to get caught in the act of this obvious self-centered narcissism. (Was it the author Edith Wharton who said the only socially acceptable part of yourself you can look at in public is your fingernails?) It's probably the same dynamic a person may experience when that person goes into a porno shop. Don't look anyone in the eye. (At least that's what they tell me.) Yet everybody *is* looking all the time . . . just surreptitious, sly glances. Everyone is looking at everyone else, they just don't get caught doing it.

It's entertaining to watch all this going on. Mirrors are all over every wall and everyone wears the workout outfits that make them and their tattoos look the best. It takes a clever person to get a glimpse of themselves in the mirror without getting caught doing it. Every now and then, however, some big muscled guy will go right up to the mirror, take off his shirt and practice flexing his muscles in the mirror. This, of course, horrifies everyone else. All taboos are being broken. The flagrant violation of it all! You're not supposed to be there to look better. Be healthier, or something like that, but not to "look better"! How embarrassing.

If you ever get caught looking at someone, if your eyes actually meet, it's a clear violation of space, a violation of an unwritten rule, and you'll *never* let yourself get caught looking at that person again. If you did, you'd have to reschedule your workouts to a different time. The only person in the gym who got directly looked at was a young woman who did her entire workout while talking on her cell phone. Everyone stared at her. She explained to one of the managers that working out was too boring.

Avoiding each other's eyes is harder than it looks. I used to play a game with my kids where I would stand sideways to them and they would stare at me. The idea was for them to try to look away before I could swing my head around and catch them looking at me. I caught them every time, and they always caught me when we changed places. On a day where there's not much going on, you might want to try this yourself.

One person I see at the fitness center every time I go there works at the local grocery store deli where she often waits on me. We talk at the store but never acknowledge each other at the center. Nor do we ever mention our dual lives when we talk at the grocery store. How strange.

The same rule holds true on the street. You may work out right next to some person for months on end, your eyes, of course, never meeting. You could probably describe his entire exercise program, but when you run into this person on the street or in a coffee shop, you look right past him. "Aren't you the guy who has worked out next to me three days a week for the past year?" "Who, me?" "Aren't you the guy I saw in the porno shop last week?" "Who, me?" People are a lot stranger than animals.

Disclaimer

Reading back over what I've written, I find it a bit mean-spirited. I must admit that there are other people at the fitness center who are there for reasons other than vanity. I have to acknowledge that I see seriously overweight people who struggle heroically to turn their lives around; and I see really old people who are probably there to feel good about themselves, to find meaning in a stronger, healthier body. One older woman who is probably in her late 70s is there on a regular basis. She has the flexibility of a 13-year-old gymnast and her body would grace a woman in her twenties. I think she must have been a dancer in her earlier days. She wears headphones and goes through a really interesting combination of stretching and working on the machines. Of course I'm watching her like I watch everybody else, but I would bet that everyone else in the center is watching her, too.

An elderly Asian woman who is a regular seems to be using the treadmill as a meditation tool. She walks at an exceptionally fast pace, no expression on her face, her eyes never moving. She stares straight ahead into a space that no one else can see, and she does this for an hour and a half at every session I have observed. She never sweats. Then she leaves.

Occasionally a person with a serious physical disability will bravely work the machines with a determination that I don't think I could ever possess. My heart goes out to these people . . . but I still won't meet their eyes.

I've also noticed that every time I see someone I know in the center, and we've not succeeded in avoiding each other's eyes, I make sure they know I'm there to heal my shoulder, leg, etc. I wouldn't want them to get the idea I'm there to get muscles. This becomes embarrassing if I forget I've already told the person about my injury and lay it all out for him again. "Why is he telling me all this again?" he asks himself. "Is he trying to hide something? I bet he flexes his muscles in his mirror at home." I am a bit oversensitive about this. I've always had a judgmental attitude about body builders, probably because I was one in my last year of college at Cal, Berkeley. In fact I got so muscled up that the gym entered me in the Mr. California contest, a contest I quickly withdrew myself from. They thought I had a good chance, but I wasn't going to admit to the world that my muscles didn't just come naturally or from honest work but from lifting a bunch of dumb weights. But I then found the muscles wouldn't go away whether I lifted weights or not. I lifted for a few months in the Marine Corps, and then hung it up. But forty years after I had lifted my last weight, people still asked me, "Where do you work out?" "I don't!" used to always be my response, coupled with a look intended to end the conversation, which I always figured was better than trying to knock them on their butt.

Another Disclaimer

A horseshoer in good condition can avoid a lot of injuries just by being strong enough to control a horse who is acting up, or by having the speed to get the hell out of there. A horseshoer who isn't in good shape will soon get in good shape if he or she keeps shoeing. However, as the shoer gets older and/or needs to cut back on the number of horses worked on, or has an injury that restricts the work, a fitness center can help keep the shoer in condition to keep on shoeing.

One good thing the center has helped me with: I can do a lot of pullups. Recently I won a Marine Corps shirt, hat, and a lanyard for my wife at the USMC booth at a local county fair for doing 21 pullups.

On the fence.

Marine Corps Mountain School. 1958. I'm on lower right.

Fresh from active duty in the Corps.

In Tacoma after active duty and before entering Seminary. 1960.

Graduating from Seminary. 1963.

Official picture of smiling Marine Corps major in Reserves. 1967.

Dad, Mom, me, and Nicky, my faithful horseshoeing dog.

Nicky, eagerly waiting in back of my truck.

Working in the sun in California. 1975.

Typical customer's view of a horseshoer.

Feeding hoof parings to wild turkeys. 1990.

Dog and turkeys eating hoof parings fresh off of horse, who couldn't care less.

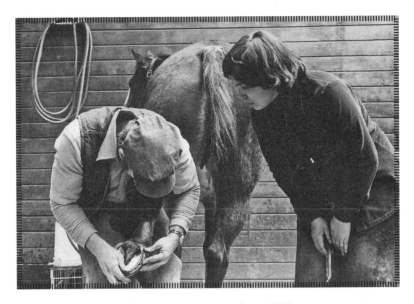

Lady apprentice watching me measure a shoe. 1978.

Rasping a foot. 2011.

Picture by David Beardsley.

Nipping for a field trim. 2011.

Picture by David Beardsley.

Cochise, my favorite customer. 2011.

Thinking about it all. 2011.

Picture by David Beardsley.

Rasping a left hind foot. 2011.

Picture by David Beardsley.

Working on a hind foot. 2011.

Picture by David Beardsley.

The trimming process. 2011.

Picture by David Beardsley.

Tools of the trade.

Picture by David Beardsley.

Tools of the trade, close up.

Picture by David Beardsley.

Working hands.

Graduating with Doctorate. 2004.

More Injuries and Violence

(Why Horseshoers Are Always Late)

The horse owner told me she wouldn't be able to meet me, but that the horse would be tied to the pasture fence. At this point, I should have been suspicious: this was a disaster-prone customer. Her horse was well behaved and a delight to shoe, but the owner was dangerous to be around. She invariably knocked over things that scared hell out of every horse in the vicinity, or ran her car into a ditch, or left a gate open for all the horses to escape . . . things like that. One time she only hurt herself. She had forgotten to catch her horse for me, and we had to drive my truck up to the top of a hill where we caught him. She should have ridden him down the hill, but chose instead to pull him beside the truck, while she sat in the cab holding his lead rope in her hand. She hoped the horse would come with us. I recommended against this. All went well until the girl enthusiastically stuck her arm out the window to wave at someone. She waved it right in her horse's face. The horse, of course, freaked out and pulled back. Instead of letting go of the rope, the girl held on as it sang through her hand. When the pain finally broke through to her disorganized mind, she let go. I stopped the truck and told her to open her hand so I could see the extent of the damage. She wouldn't open it. Half an hour later, I was able to convince her to open it, both of us expecting a half-inch-deep bloody groove through the middle of her palm. The damage was minimal, however, and I patched it up with my ever-ready first aid kit. Not that it matters in the long run, but all of this cost me an extra hour and caused me to be an hour late to my next appointment where the owner petulantly asked me why it was that horseshoers were always late.

Back to the story. As I said, I should have been suspicious. When I got to the stable, I could immediately see her horse. It was the horse tied to the fence, the fence torn down by the horse who was tied to it not by the usual halter and lead rope but by a lasso tied around his neck, a lasso that had tightened and was strangling the horse. Ten or fifteen other horses were standing right there so fascinated by the spectacle that they didn't notice the fence was broken down and that they all could have escaped. The choking horse was wild-eyed and standing with all four feet spread out, desperately trying to breathe. I didn't know how long this had been going on.

I cautiously approached the horse, talking in what I thought was a soothing voice in hope of calming him down. But soothing voices don't have much of a calming effect on a horse who is strangling to death. I don't think he even knew I was there. The rope was so tight that the only way to free him would be to cut the rope, but each time I got close, the horse broke into another wild frenzy, further tightening the rope around his neck. The other horses were enthralled.

So was Michael, the fourteen-year-old developmentally disabled boy I had brought along as a favor to his parents.

They wanted him to enjoy a day in the country with some lovely horses and farm animals and a friendly horseshoer as a guide. Michael was unusual. Completely deaf and mostly blind, his main joy in life was to sit with his face almost pressed against a TV screen and watch fights, car wrecks, and other scenes of violence at which he screamed and shouted with delight, throwing himself around the room, shouting and yelling and knocking things over, then running back to press against the TV again, as if to recharge his batteries.

Michael was standing next to me as I approached the desperate horse and immediately realized he was about to experience the high point of his life of watching violence. The first time the horse jerked violently and went into its throes of panic, Michael was ecstatic. He shrieked with laughter and started jumping up and down, running all around the horse. I couldn't tell him to stop, he was deaf.

I finally got a hold on Michael and firmly placed him back in the truck. I was able to cut the rope before the horse choked to death, and I was able to chase the thoroughly entertained bunch of horses back into the pasture long enough to temporarily tie the fence back up. It took another 45 minutes to calm the almost strangled horse down before I could even think of trying to shoe him, but I eventually got shoes on him without injuring either one of us. All of this caused me to be about an hour late to my next customer, another person who found it interesting that horseshoers are always late. Someone should invent a telephone you can carry around with you to call ahead when you're delayed. (They already have?)

Ponies

Ponies, mostly because they are small, aren't able to cause the kinds of wrecks that horses do, and they generally maintain a lower profile than horses, probably because they are smarter and don't want anyone to know it. If you look closely at a pony you might notice that he or she is looking back at you just as closely, calculating just how much they can get away with. They are figuring out whether to fight or just give up and let you trim their feet or put on the inevitable shoes. But it's never a good idea to turn your back on a pony. There are a lot of gentle little ponies, of course, but some ponies can hold a grudge for a long time and if of a vengeful mind will let fly a kick when least expected. I've seen a lot of this kind.

One pony I trimmed a few times was on the string of riding horses at a Boy Scout camp in the mountains of Northern California. This pony was a full-out fighter when it came time for his feet to be trimmed. I could do nothing with him unless I tied up each leg to be worked on. I used a big soft rope and even after the foot was safely off the ground he still jumped and bucked and twisted around until completely worn out. Somehow he always managed to keep enough balance to avoid falling, something a horse in similar circumstances would not be able to do. I would just watch until he had worn himself out. I took some pictures with my little camera, but you can hardly make anything out because of the clouds of dust he raised. I thought this was just a vicious animal who should be sent somewhere else, but the head wrangler, a feisty twenty-year-old kid, said the pony was always gentle with the boys on his back. He had never been anything but a model steed for his small riders.

One day the discussion between the wrangler and me kept being interrupted by Billy, a loud, active seven-year-old Scout who was running all over the barn and seriously getting on the nerves of the wrangler. "This kid drives me nuts!" complained the wrangler. "He's always into everything and he's determined to spend his entire day in here with me. He climbs into the stalls and scares the hell out of the horses, he chases the cats back and forth across the barn, and he throws dirt clods at anything that moves." The boy's behavior bothered the wrangler more than it did me because I couldn't see how anything could get worse than the wild pony I had to deal with.

The next time I came to shoe the riding string and trim the pony, the wrangler had an idea he wanted to try out on me. He was sure his plan for the pony would work, but looking back on it I don't think he would have cared that much if it hadn't worked. His plan: "This pony gives all you farriers nothing but trouble when you try to trim him, but he's really gentle with the boys. Why not put one of them on his back while you're trimming him? I'm sure he won't give you any trouble then because he won't want to hurt the boy." He looked thoughtful for a moment, and then said, "Why don't we use Billy?" I didn't think sacrificing Billy was too good an idea, but after the wrangler promised to hold firmly onto Billy while he was on the pony's back, and that in no way would I be liable, I decided to give it a try. Stranger things have been attempted. Billy was ecstatic, of course, and sat up there like the perfect rider. It worked. The pony didn't move a muscle while I trimmed his feet with a boy on his back. We successfully used that method from then on.

Welsh Ponies

Welsh ponies are marvelous examples of independent thinking. I have two favorite stories about the mindset you might expect to find in a Welsh pony. These little animals are not necessarily stubborn or mean, but they do get their point across. In both of these stories, the owners were seldom there. I just set up a regular shoeing schedule and showed up every eight weeks, shod the ponies, and left a bill that was always promptly paid.

My first Welsh example was a pleasant little pony who was impossible to catch. Once I caught him he was a joy to work with, but catching him was something else. The owner had warned me about this, but in those days I had unwarranted confidence in my ability to catch anything. That first day the pony and I probably spent an hour walking around each other. He always kept just out of reach, obviously enjoying himself. I finally gave up, got my rope out of the truck and lassoed him. The next time I came out I figured he knew I could catch him, and being an intelligent animal would quietly give up and just stand there while I haltered him. I was wrong. This trip I wasted little time chasing him around the field, but went to my truck, got out the rope and lassoed him again. For several months I carried the rope out with me and seeing it in my hand he just stood there and let me walk up and catch him. We did this for about a year, at which time I figured I had him trained. But the day I went out to get him without the rope, he walked away from me again. Ten minutes later I tired of the old game and went after the rope. Of course he stood quietly when I approached with that rope in hand.

I shod this pony for seven years. Every few months I tried catching him without the rope in my hand and it never worked. He never ran but just kept out of reach. He seemed to enjoy this so much that I decided to play the game once or twice a year when I would go out without the rope. I'm sure he looked forward to these times when we could spend a pleasant ten minutes or so walking all over the field before I got the rope to end the game. I really missed this guy after he died.

Another Welsh pony in the same rural neighborhood was easy to catch and a perfect gentleman to put shoes on. I never tied him up to anything but would just catch him and leave him standing in the front yard eating the grass while I worked on him. One time, however, I burned my hand on the forge and angrily stomped over to try the shoe on. The pony moved away to get at a better clump of grass and, for the first time ever, I yelled at him. He stopped eating, turned to look at me with a beady eye and disdainfully walked off. Down the street he went. I just stood there, knowing that if I went after him he would just keep on going. About a mile down the road he stopped and looked back at me standing there with a horseshoe in my hand. I guess he figured I had been punished enough and he turned and ambled back. He stood quietly eating grass while I finished the job. I never yelled at him again.

The next two stories aren't so much about the ponies as they are about the owners.

One day in Northern California, while shoeing a horse, I noticed a lady intently watching me. When I had finished the horse and was putting my tools back in the truck, the lady walked up to me and announced that I appeared to know what I was doing and would I come down to her place and look at her pony's feet. She wasn't sure if he needed any work done or not, but wanted my opinion. She lived just down the road so I said I'd stop by. She said the pony wouldn't come to us so we had to walk out in the field to look at him. When I got there I immediately understood why he wouldn't walk. His feet looked like elf boots, curled up to where the toe had turned back to touch the leg. It was the worst case of founder I had ever seen.

I didn't have the time to trim him that day, but I made an appointment to come back in a few days. On a job that usually took about twenty minutes, it took me an hour and a half to trim those feet down close to normal. I had to use a hacksaw, although a chainsaw or an axe would probably have been better tools for the job.

The lady turned out to be a nice person who was concerned about her pony and her other animals, but knew almost nothing about caring for them. She put her pony completely in my hands and said to do whatever was necessary whenever it was needed. The founder was so advanced that a five-week trimming schedule was scarcely enough to keep the growth down. Eventually I got the feet under control so he could move around comfortably.

The hot, dry summers, however, brought another problem. One hot day in August I went out for his regular trim and couldn't make even the first cut. The feet were like rocks. I had dealt with a lot of hard feet, but had never experienced anything like this, and felt like a wimp for giving up on him and going home. I called the lady and asked her to let the water trough overflow and tie him so he would be standing in water all night. She did this and the next morning his feet had softened up enough to trim. He was my only customer who ever needed that treatment. He lived to be 22 years old.

At another shoeing I noticed a stern-looking older woman, her gray hair in a tight bun, glaring at me. I was sure I hadn't crippled her horse or insulted her daughter or anything else to warrant those stares, but it did get on my nerves. When I was finished with the horse she approached me and regally stated that I had passed her intense and knowledgeable evaluation of my work and that I was, therefore, qualified to look at the problem her new pony was having with his feet. Warning signals popped up all around me, but I said I would look at her pony and we set an appointment for the following week. When I arrived at her house, she questioned me again about my training and experience, explaining that she was a serious horseperson who would not tolerate shoddy work by an unqualified farrier. Eventually convinced that I was a competent horseshoer, she went on to describe the situation with her pony. She had recently purchased the animal, who was of good stock, and she was concerned that the feet needed work because the pony wouldn't walk. With effort she could lead him, but he would walk nowhere on his own. The animal was for her granddaughter, a qualified rider, and the pony needed to be in the best of condition.

Promising only to give my evaluation, I walked with the lady to look at the problem. The pony was quietly standing by a barn wall with his head hanging down. Expecting overgrown feet, I was surprised to see that they looked recently trimmed. Maybe it was an infection or a nail in the frog, the soft center part of the foot. (Two days before, I had pulled a hidden nail out of another horse's foot, immediately followed by a blast of pus and blood.) I picked up all four feet and found nothing. I could have saved myself this effort if I had looked at the pony's face before I looked at the feet. His eyes had this light glaze over them, and when I moved my hand near them, they didn't react. He was stone blind.

I straightened up and formally announced that there was nothing wrong with the pony's feet. I suggested to the horsewoman that perhaps a vet could determine what the trouble was, thanked her for consulting me, and left. No charge.

Insensitivity?

Some customers are more insensitive than others. One particular gentleman called for an appointment for two shoeings. When I asked how the horses behaved, he said, "Well, you can pick up their feet." That should have been a gigantic red flag to me, but being short of cash, I said I would come out there.

I drive for an hour and a half through some delightful woods and hills and arrive right on time. The ranch is large and well kept. There is a huge barn and a lot of tractors and other farm machinery around the barn and the house. A trampoline is beside the barn. My only greeters, however, are a serious-looking Bull Mastiff who is not wagging his tail, and three barefoot children whose ages turn out to be two, four, and six, who have been jumping on the unsupervised trampoline. Two girls and an older boy. No adults in sight. I do not get out of the truck. The three children and the dog stare at me. I'm obviously some kind of novelty. I wait. Our conversation doesn't seem to be going anywhere, and the dog has not taken his eyes off of me. I finally ask the boy to go get his mother. He gives it some thought, and finally wanders off in the direction of the house. Eventually, his mother comes back with him, and all four of them and the dog stare at me. The mother turns out to be the daughter of the man who called me, but she knows nothing about any of this. She has no idea who I am or where her father is. I tell her I'm the shoer.

I work up some courage and start rattling the door handle like I'm going to be getting out. I open the door a little, keeping my legs inside and my eyes on the dog. He continues to stare. I close the door. The mother just stands there looking at me. She doesn't invite me to get out of the truck. The dog walks off.

OK. One hurdle removed. The mother of the three kids, who was probably waiting for the dog's judgment of me, tells me to get out of the truck and we walk over to look at the two horses. They both have brand-new shoes on. The mother said they didn't have any shoes on a few days ago. She is vaguely puzzled. Not concerned, just vaguely puzzled.

I look off into the hills for a while. Then I remember the man who called me said he also had two mini horses who needed trimming. When I gave him my rates for trimming, he said it was too much. I said if those mini horses didn't give me too much trouble I would probably do them at a discount since I would be out there anyway. Now I decide to trim them and charge him full price . . . if the daughter will pay me. The daughter has no money. I will take a post-dated check. OK.

I pick up a couple of halters and go out to get the mini horses who turn out to be Shetland ponies, one of which is a stud. They see me coming and head out over the hills. I am determined to come out of this thing with some money. I eventually entice them into the small paddock by rattling some hay in a bucket, amazed that they fall for that. While trying to catch the mare, I look over to see the two-year-old and the four-year-old girls standing right next to me. They have slipped through the fence. I tell them to please leave. The stud does not like any of this and is running all over the little paddock. The girls head toward the gate where I have left my tools. The two-year-old picks up my nippers. She could chop off a finger by just looking at those lethal things. I yell. They drop the tools and rush out of the gate.

I finally catch both ponies. Their feet are fairly short and don't really need a trim. I do them anyway. Full price. I pick up my post-dated check and leave.

I do not expect a call of apology and I don't get one. My wife says I should charge the man full price for two shoeings. Some shoers would.

Flies

Closely related to horses and ponies are, of course, flies. They come with the territory. On a nice warm day a deposit of fresh horse turds will have a thousand flies on it before it hits the ground. I think the flies watch the horse and know when he's ready to let go, then mill around the exit and grab hold on the way down, fighting for the best spots. Some experts say the fly larvae live in the horse's bowels and spring to life when the manure lands in the dirt. I doubt that the fly larvae cause much distress to the horse from inside, but once outside, the battle begins, and the horseshoer is right in the middle.

I certainly don't pretend to know anything technical or scientific about flies, but from my position at ground level, I can describe several kinds and I will tell some stories about each and the battle waged against them by horse and shoer.

The most prominent buzzing nemesis looks like a regular housefly, and for all I know, it is. These flies don't give up easily. They generally swarm around the feet and ankles of the horse and sometimes get so engrossed (an appropriate word) in the often bloody feast that you can squash them right on the horse. If you wave them off, they rise about an inch and jump right back on. These flies won't bother a leg that is being held by the shoer, but that leaves three other legs for them to assault. And that's where the trouble starts. There is no way an average horse is going to stand quietly with one foot in the shoer's lap and three feet on the ground being eaten by flies. You can yell and shout and insult the horse for wriggling around, but the horse is simply not going to stand still under this kind of fly attack. All of this limits the options for the shoer. Assuming there is no fly spray (more about that later), the shoer will probably try to get as much work done as possible on a foot before the horse reaches the limits of its tolerance and breaks loose, scattering horseshoer and tools.

Sometimes these kinds of flies settle on the horse's stomach and sometimes on the face. The flies on the stomach can at least be periodically re-arranged when the horse whips his tail around, but even this can cause some grief to the shoer because when your head is down working on a foot, the tail will slap you right in the face. It feels like a whip. That's why shoers always wear baseball hats or hats with a good brim to ward off the blows from the tail. A brief aside: I was once asked to testify in court as a defense witness for a customer who was falsely accused of managing a dirty barn. Part of the accusation referred to flies being everywhere. This was not true. His barn was incredibly clean, with almost no flies at all, and I was well aware of this. While on the stand, I was asked by the opposing attorney how I could substantiate that there were no flies. My response was that his barn was the only working facility where I did not wear a hat. My bald head was safe from fly attack and I didn't need to protect my face from the horses' tails because there were no flies to be swished away. My testimony, according to the attorney, won the case for my customer. It also caused a lot of laughter.

If these kinds of flies are not controlled, the shoer needs to be cautious not only about being hit in the face with the tail, but also about getting kicked in the head. This is how you can get kicked in the head: if you are working on a hind foot while it's on the hoof stand, you are putting your head directly in a position to get kicked if the horse kicks back with a front foot to chase flies off his stomach. This happened to me only once. I got a foot right in the middle of the forehead that knocked me back about five feet. I still have the scar.

The best control for these flies is fly spray or a liquid fly wipe. A lot of shoers carry their own fly spray because it is almost impossible to work on a horse who is being harassed by flies. The problem here is that a spray that works perfectly one summer may not work at all the next summer because, I am convinced, the flies adjust to it. It's like they have little laboratories where fly scientists are rapidly developing antidotes for each new fly spray that comes to market. It's frustrating to discover the perfect spray only to find it completely useless within a year's time. Even with brand new cans. I used to make my own fly spray out of Hexol and water and a secret ingredient that worked for two years. I was really pleased, but it, too, eventually failed. The flies were on to me.

One time I was working in a huge modern barn, and was sitting on my tailgate taking a coffee break when a fine mist began drifting down from overhead. I asked the ranch foreman what that was, and he said it was the automatic fly spray disseminator. I immediately put my hand over my coffee cup, but he told me not to worry about it. "That stuff won't hurt you," he said. "You can drink it. It's made from some kind of African Chrysanthemum that kills flies but doesn't harm people." I thanked him for the information and kept my hand over my cup.

There's a story that goes around, most likely a rural myth, about a horseshoer who was so bothered by the horse's tail slapping him that he tied a big hammer to the tail to hold it down. Of course the horse swung the tail and the hammer around and knocked the shoer out cold. Interesting, but probably not true.

The worst cases of fly assault I've ever seen have been upon donkeys and burros who have skinny little legs that seem to have a special attraction to flies. If left unchecked, the flies and even bees, will eat the skin right off the legs and then go for the blood and serum that leaks out. These little animals don't seem as bothered by the flies as are the horses, but without treatment donkeys and burros can become crippled by what looks like a simple housefly.

In summer I used to leave the windows open on my truck while working and flies would fill the cab. I could determine the density of the fly population for that particular day by timing how long it took for the last of the flies to blow out my windows as I drove off. A relatively fly-free day would have them out within five minutes. A heavy fly day would require up to twenty-five minutes. Sometimes my friends tell me to get a life.

Another type, Bott flies, are curious little things with some kind of underslung protuberance. They hover around the front parts of horses looking like a refueling airplane with its hanging fuel hose. They are looking for a nice place to deposit their little yellow eggs. They prefer the front legs of the horse because the idea is that the horse will lick its legs and the eggs will be transported to the horse's intestines where they grow into more Bott flies so they can do it all over again. These flies are not much of an external bother to horse or shoer. They can be easily swatted out of the air, but because their eggs end up in the horse's bowels, they are more dangerous to the horse's health than all other types of flies.

The smallest fly, not much bigger than a gnat, is a biter. Very early in my career I was shoeing a horse who was jiggling and dancing around. I could see the little flies on him, but I thought they were too small to be causing such distress to the horse. So I smacked the horse and yelled at him to stop jumping around. "These flies aren't bothering you," I accused. "You're just using them as an excuse to misbehave." Then one of them bit me. I suddenly understood and apologized to the horse.

There are two other kinds of flies that work alone rather than in swarms. Some people have called one or the other of them "horse flies," but I have never been sure what they are. One of them is long and sleek and gray, like a steel rocket. These are a bit larger than houseflies and will grab ahold of a horse and draw blood. They are speedy and sneaky. You can't kill them because you can't catch them, and they couldn't care less about fly spray. The best thing to do when they show up is to step back and try to reason with them. Maybe if they are free to get one drink they will leave peacefully. Otherwise it's best to just leave and come back another day. The horses will not tolerate these flies and not much can be done about them.

Even worse . . . the big black and yellow bomber fly. These, also rare, are slower but much more threatening to the horse. They lumber in, almost shoving the shoer aside, land on the horse's back and take a big bite. I don't think they drink blood; they just eat the flesh. And they pay no attention to efforts to chase them off. I have knocked them out of the air, stepped on them, and watched them shake themselves off and fly away. About the only way to kill these flies is to put them on the anvil and hit them a couple of good blows with the hammer. If that doesn't kill them, it usually will discourage them.

These flies will cause so much terror in the horses that they often will forget all of their irritating little behavior issues when one of these flies is in the neighborhood. I remember working on a flighty, nervous, extremely irritating little horse who was giving me all kinds of trouble by pretending to be horrified by every move I made. If I scratched my nose, the horse would freak. If I reached up to adjust my hat, the horse was certain I was going to kill it. If I was so audacious as to try to pick up a foot, the horse would try to break loose and run off. All of this nonsense came to an illuminating stop, however, when one of these big black and yellow flies landed on the horse's back. I stepped back and took off my hat to try to swat the fly. The horse knew what I was about to do. He stood quietly shaking, teeth chattering, while I slammed my hat down on the fly in an attempt to discourage it. The horse stood quietly and was obviously relieved when the fly was gone. The game was over. Knowing his behavior had been exposed as a big fake, he settled down and stood quietly for the rest of the shoeing.

The Marin County Rodeo

I've shod horses at a lot of rodeos over the years, and I've always been impressed with how professional they are, even the "amateur" ones. Good stock contractors like John Growney (Growney Brothers), and Cotton Rosser, out here in the West, are what make these rodeos as good as they are. These boys know what they're doing, and they're respected throughout the rodeo world.

But one rodeo stands out in my mind. It took place, or I should say tried to take place, on the Civic Center grounds in Marin County, California.

Some local promoter of music concerts thought this small yuppy community might pay to see a real rodeo with real horses and cows and bulls, and everything. (Actually, the term "yuppy" had not been invented yet, but I can't remember the official name we called yuppies in 1976.) There were a few ranches and horses in Marin, but they were mostly out on the edges of this county where no bad smells or flies could drift into the sophisticated suburban designer home neighborhoods.

The promoter called me to ask if I would be available to shoe some horses. I said I would and agreed to meet him. Over a cup of coffee, he told me he had never even seen a rodeo. But he had a big new black cowboy hat, a bolo tie with a big chunk of turquoise, and an expensive new pair of Justin cowboy boots. He thought a rodeo would be quite an experience for the BMW set, so he started to put one together. He knew the first thing he needed was a place to hold it. There was a lot of undeveloped land behind the Civic Center that looked like a good place to him, and being a big shot in the community, he was given permission to use those grounds. He asked around and was told that he would need fencing for the perimeter of the grounds, stock pens for the animals, gates and chutes, portable stands for the audience, and a ticket booth. He would also need a bunch of animals. He contracted with several outfits to get the equipment, and he brought in a local with a tractor to prepare the arena grounds. He found a guy who said he would deliver all the livestock needed to put on a good rodeo.

The promoter may have been a genius at putting on music concerts, but he had a lot to learn about rodeos. The first new thing he learned was that you need more than three days to prepare for a rodeo. And you need to coordinate things like arrival time of the stock and arrival time of the pens to house them. The stock arrived on the scene one whole day before the pens did, so the animals spent a few more hours in trailers and cattle carriers than they had expected. Not the best accommodations. When the pens did arrive, no one quite understood how to set them up. For awhile there were cattle and horses wandering in and out of opened gates into each other's pens, looking for old friends and to see what everyone else was eating. When the promoter and his "hands" finally got the pens set up, they had put bulls in with the mothers of the calves used in the calf roping events, and the calves in with bucking horses and some roping steers, and just about every other kind of housing disaster you could imagine.

While the stock visited with each other, a group of high school kids picked huge rocks out of the proposed arena, and some workers tried to set up a fence to surround the rodeo grounds. This was all happening on the opening day of the rodeo. It was scheduled to start at three o'clock that afternoon.

The commotion created by this activity began to attract a lot of curious people. By this time, the portable stands had been set up and that's where they went to sit and watch. The ticket booth and ticket seller were in place, ready to go, but since the fences weren't up, people just wandered in from all directions and sat in the stands. By the time the fence was in place and the ticket booth in operation, the stands already had about a hundred people sitting and enjoying the spectacle.

The spectacle they were enjoying was mostly the 50 high school kids who were rushing around the arena picking up rocks the size of cantaloupes and throwing them over the fence into what was to be the parking lot. A tractor was trying to drag the arena, but all it was doing was turning up more big rocks. The promoter was yelling at the kids to direct them toward rocks they had missed, while the rodeo contestants stood on the edges of the arena staring in disbelief at the rocks. About this time I was torn away from all the fun and put to work taking off horseshoes, putting heavy plastic protective pads on the horses' feet, and replacing the shoes. The barrel racing girls lined up, all of them pleading with me to hurry. They were not going to risk their horses' feet stepping on big rocks without some kind of protection.

As it turned out, my work wasn't really needed because none of the barrel racers actually ran their horses around the barrels: they walked them. The winning time was something like 30 seconds, a new world record for slow. About a third of the girls carefully walked as fast as they could, steering their horses around the rocks, while another third just sat up smiling self-consciously at the crowd and let their horses wend their own way through the rock field. The remaining third had already packed it in and were loading up their horses to go home or move on to the next rodeo, vowing never to return to Marin County, California.

These disgruntled girls weren't the only ones to drive off in a rage. A whole contingent of cowboys had roared off in clouds of dust before the rodeo even got started. Several ropers told me they were not going to risk their horses with all those rocks, and a few cowboys in the riding events told me they weren't going to risk their own heads on those rocks. A bull rider I talked with was particularly upset. He had driven down from Montana for what he thought was going to be a big California rodeo. He took one look at the rocks in the arena and went over to try to get his entry fees back. Good luck.

The barrel racing wasn't the only yawner event that afternoon. The bucking events were equally exciting. Two of the bulls burst out of the chutes with riders on their backs and ran straight across the arena and smashed into the fence. The riders might have gotten a good score in the bull running event, but not in bucking. A third bull just took his rider for a casual eight-second walk around the arena. That didn't rate a very good score, either. The horses weren't much better. Some bucked, others just wandered around with a puzzled rider on their backs. No one in charge had ever heard of a re-ride.

The most exciting part of the rodeo was when a bull jumped over the flimsy barricade and ran past my truck parked there. I was sitting in the cab watching the rodeo, and several people were standing at the fence. After the bull ran by, 13 people were standing in the bed of my pickup.

I don't remember where the stock came from, probably from a local ranch or some riding stable. Apparently someone had connections, however, because that stock was all moved out that evening and reputable stock contractor Cotton Rosser brought his animals in for the next two days. Cotton knew what he was doing. He set everything up the way it should have been. He brought in a big crew and some effective machinery to clear up the rocks in the arena. He re-arranged the pens, and tried to convince some of the disgruntled cowboys and cowgirls to stay on for the next two days. Because of his reputation, a lot of them did, and things went well for the remainder of the rodeo.

I never did understand how that transfer was made so smoothly and so quickly. Maybe Cotton Rosser had already been scheduled for the Saturday and Sunday performances, and our music promoter in his black cowboy hat talked his way into handling the Friday evening performance. He was a good talker. Regardless, there are a lot of cowboys and cowgirls out there who will probably have nothing to do with Marin County to this day.

The Newspaper Reporter

After I had been shoeing about twelve years, a newspaper reporter in Northern California who had heard about me from someone, called to set up an interview. He was interested in my background prior to taking up horseshoeing, and wanted to write an article about that. That was all right with me, and we set up a time when I could be doing a horse so he could observe the process.

I had already started working on the horse when the reporter showed up in his big blue news truck and walked over to the horse and me in his fancy loafers and his reporter's hat. He had no notepad or pencil, no tape recorder or any other note-taking device. We shook hands. "Is this the horse?" he asked. I looked at him a moment. "Yes." "Oh," he said, and just stood there. I said nothing and continued working. Silence. After awhile he asked, "Do you like your work?" I said yes I did. More silence. After a few more minutes he asked, "Is this a hard job?" Once again I stopped. I put my tools down and looked directly at him. "Yes, it is," I announced. We looked at each other for a moment, and I went back to work, telling myself that this was the poorest excuse for a reporter I had ever seen, and as far as I was concerned, the interview was over.

So I began talking to the horse and my dog. The reporter could listen in if he wanted to. I blabbed on.

When I was done with the horse, the reporter and I shook hands again, wished each other a good day, and parted company. As far as I was concerned, that was the end of it. I was surprised when later that week, the story about "The Horseshoer" came out in a feature article in the local paper. It was an incredible story. I was amazed. He had obviously set me up to ignore his presence and just talk about whatever came into my mind. I read about all the stuff I had told the horse and my dog. I guess he had been listening and memorizing. He never took a single note, but he got everything right. I called him later to tell him how impressed I was, and to apologize for my premature opinion of him. He laughed and said that's how it's done.

That paper had a large circulation and I expected a bunch of new customers from the article. As far as I know, I never got even one. What I did get was eight people who called to tell me how disillusioned and bored they were in their jobs and asking if I would take them on as apprentices. I said no to them all.

The Bad Job?

I thought I had done a bad job on one particular horse I shod in Northern California. A quite pleasant lady had called to set up an appointment to shoe her mare. She said she would meet me at the pasture because she was the only one who could catch the mare. She told me the horse was easy to shoe, just hard to catch.

I showed up on the appointed date and was pleased to see that the horse was, in fact, easy to shoe. I enjoyed talking with the lady, and I enjoyed shoeing her horse. I figured I had done a good job. I gave my usual suggestion to the owner that the shoeing should be done every eight weeks. With my regular customers I always pull out my appointment book and schedule the next visit, but with new customers I hesitate to do that in case they decide they don't like my work and don't want me back in eight weeks. I'll wait for them to call me. I told her she should call me, or some other shoer, around that time to pull off the shoes and either trim and put new shoes on, or just trim the feet. If you leave the shoes on past eight weeks, the feet will just keep growing and the horse might go lame. She said she would call me.

The eight weeks came and went and I heard nothing from the lady. I don't like to call back my customers unless we have a definite schedule, so I just waited a bit longer. Another month passed and I finally decided she just didn't like the job I did, and I wrote her off as a dissatisfied customer.

Six months later I got a call from her asking me to come out to remove the shoes and trim the mare. She didn't want shoes this time. I was pleased to hear from her again, and figured she had used another shoer, didn't like him, and was coming back to me. That was good. I asked her when would be a good time for us to meet at the horse, but she told me to just go out to the same place, catch the horse and trim her. She would mail me a check. I asked her how I was supposed to catch the horse. She said, "You won't have any problem. The mare just stands out in one spot in that field all day. You can walk right up to her." OK. I'll give it a try.

A few days later I drove out to the pasture and saw the mare standing out in the field like the lady said. This time, however, there was a baby about three months old standing beside her. Cautiously I walked out toward them. The mare didn't move. If she had taken two steps away from me, I would have just left. I had seen how hard it was for the owner to catch her, and I knew if she took off I wouldn't stand a chance of catching her in that five-acre pasture.

The horse didn't move. I approached as carefully as I could, reached out and put my halter on her. The baby had no idea what was going on. I started to lead the mare over to a fence where I could tie her, but she wouldn't move. Then I looked at her feet. I recognized the shoes I had put on six months ago. This was a shock to me since shoes normally will fall off after three months, sometimes even before the eight weeks are up. Her feet, like elf boots, were all curled up at the toe. She didn't move because the strain on her tendons would have seriously pained her. She would have had to walk on the backs of her heels. I didn't know why the lady hadn't called. Sometimes people have no concept of time and think it's eight weeks when it's actually two or three months. But, six months? This horse could easily have been crippled. I suspected the reason she didn't meet me at the field was because she was embarrassed at having seriously neglected her horse. Or, she could have been clueless. I never found out, because I moved away to Oregon shortly after.

I realized that I could take those shoes off and trim the feet right where she was standing, and that's what I did. A normal trim doesn't take much longer than fifteen or twenty minutes, but this one took over an hour. The mare stood quietly the entire time, with the baby standing beside her, always on the other side from the one I was working on.

When I was finished, I took off the halter and stepped back. She still didn't move. I gave her a little push and she took a step. Another push, another step. She began to realize her feet were back to normal, took a few more tentative steps, walked slowly in a circle around the baby and me, and then took off at a full gallop. She tore around the field on that sunny day while the baby and I stood staring after her. I knew what was going on, but the baby had probably never seen his mother move before, and had no idea what was happening. He soon got the idea, however, and raced after his mother. I watched them both tear around that field for about half an hour. It was really beautiful.

A Different Kind of Bad Job

Once in awhile you run into really unpleasant people and situations in horseshoeing. I remember one in Oregon that still makes my blood boil. A barn manager I knew called me to shoe a horse who belonged to some new lady who had obviously been neglecting that animal. The barn manager was a responsible person and he was not going to tolerate neglect. He didn't care that the woman had not asked to have the job done; he would add the cost of the shoeing to her barn bill. When I arrived at the barn, I was aghast at the condition of the feet. They hadn't been touched for probably close to a year and were spread out so badly that it would be almost impossible to keep a shoe on. The foot had the consistency of a cantaloupe. Placing a horseshoe on the foot was like putting a cup down in the center of a big plate, the cup being the shoe and the plate being the foot. The foot should have been the size of the cup, not the size of the plate. In my opinion, that woman had abused her horse.

This all happened about ten years after the situation in the previous section with the mare and her baby, and by the time of this Oregon story I had developed a pretty good

144

instinct about how people cared for their horses. I believe the lady in Northern California loved her horse. I don't think she knew much about horses, and she probably just didn't keep track of time. This lady in Oregon, I'm convinced, couldn't have cared less about her horse. He was gaunt and uncared for, and his feet were a disaster. The lady should have been turned into the Humane Society.

I did what I could, trying to compromise between the correct shoe size and the unnaturally spread out and over-sized foot. I put the nails in the best places I could find and I trimmed off as much excess as I could. I knew I would need to go back in three or four weeks to pull those shoes and reposition them because I knew the nails wouldn't hold longer than three or four weeks because of the spongy consistency of the feet.

About two weeks later, I got a call from the barn manager telling me that the lady said I had done a shitty job and that I should come out and do it over again, for free. I went out and looked at the shoes. The nails were somewhat loose, as they would be after being in a cantaloupe for two weeks, so I pulled the shoes, re-shod the horse, and told the barn manager to tell the owner to go to hell. I knew this was going to be another case of someone bad-mouthing me wherever they went, but I didn't care.

This all happened a number of years ago, and as I write this I am wondering why I have chosen this particular incident to describe. It's not as if I had never done a shitty job before. (About a month into the business I had done a girl's horse just before Christmas, and on Christmas day she called to inform me that all four shoes had come off after two weeks. They had been pulled off in the mud. I had not done a good job. I spent three hours on that Christmas day replacing the shoes.) I think the attitude and behavior of the customer is what makes the difference. The incident with the lady from the barn doesn't seem like such a big deal as I read it over, but there's still a lot of anger on my part. I'm not sure why. I might need to study on this a bit. I might learn something.

Crime in a Small Town

I live in the rural Northwest, where, contrary to popular belief, a small town can have problems with crime. I'm going to tell about some of them.

Before I get into the actual crimes we have to deal with here, I need to mention one curious thing. We don't seem to have many problems with kids or teenagers. It's an odd experience to walk up to a 17-year-old kid whose hair is sticking straight up in multi-colored spikes, his body covered with tattoos, his head filled with metal piercings, and ask him how to get to the nearest Starbucks, and he responds pleasantly and eagerly, even calling you "sir." This usually happens. And the kid isn't playing you for a fool; it's the way the kids act around here. I never got that kind of response in California. Another thing that may have something to do with kids is that there never seems to be any graffiti anywhere, even on bathroom walls in gas stations. This is pretty much true throughout the area. The biggest graffiti I've seen is on the walls of a tunnel where the culprits use a wet towel to write their messages in the grime on the tunnel walls. The messages will say something like, "I love you Sarah," "Support the Queen of the Netherlands," or "US out of Oregon." The messages last only a few days, however, because the cleanup crews wash down the walls frequently.

But each week the police report in the local paper lists some car break-ins where stereos and such are stolen. Granted, most of these are because the car wasn't locked, but some are actually "break-ins." Occasionally we even have something stolen from a house, usually because the doors were not locked, or a window was left open, but serious, nevertheless.

A few months ago, I was an unwitting participant in one of the more violent criminal acts. I had just finished shoeing some horses and had stopped at our local Mom and Pop restaurant for a hamburger and milkshake. My wife was with me and we began to wonder why the milkshake was taking so long. We finally asked the waitress, who told us that they had run out of milk and had to send the cook to the store to get some, and she was still at the store because her ex-husband had shown up at the same time and had pulled his rifle out of his truck and was threatening to shoot her when she came out of the store with our milk. The police were trying to talk the ex-husband out of it, but the guy was a stubborn sort and it might be some time before we got the milk to make our milk shake. We had finished our hamburgers by this time and decided to forget the milkshake and go look at the standoff, but it was all settled by the time we got there. I guess everyone said they were sorry and it wouldn't happen again, and they all parted on good terms. Pretty exciting while it lasted, however.

As if that wasn't crime enough, a few months later we were actually on the site of an attempted shoplifting. Apparently a young woman had tried to steal something from the Longs drugstore and was spotted in the act by a plainclothes policeman who caught her outside and was trying to put her on the ground to handcuff her. She was shouting for help, and yelling that she was being attacked. Of course this caused several bystanders led by an old gentleman to rush to her assistance demanding to know what the man was doing and ready to attack him in her defense. The beleaguered cop struggled to get his badge out with one hand and control the woman with the other. He kept yelling, "Stand back, sir!" which had no effect at all. I guess he was probably some big city cop unacquainted with the independent and determined ways of the locals. After a few tense moments and careful scrutiny of his badge, the ominous crowd stepped back. We didn't get to see the conclusion of this event because our truck was right in the middle of the whole thing and we had to drive on. Of course it made the headlines in the next week's paper.

That's about all the crime I can think of for now, except for the time someone threw a pop can at our house, and, oh yeah, someone keeps flipping our mailbox open.

The Bird Man

One of the nicest customers I ever worked for was a young Scottish man who had been in the United States for only a few years. He came from a moneyed family, I think, because he owned a large estate with 50 acres for his two horses and pony to run on, and his only occupation seemed to be the rescue operation he maintained on his property for wild birds. He had eagles, owls, swans, hawks, ducks, and a lot of birds I didn't recognize. They were brought to him by agencies and individuals from all over the state of California, and he spent most of his time putting splints on wings and performing other kinds of doctoring. He loved his work and was devoted to every bird in his charge. We always planned to spend more time at his ranch than at most places, because we enjoyed listening to his stories about each bird and how it had come into his care. He smiled a lot, was a careful and courteous listener, and was that rare person who when he asked how you were doing, really wanted to know.

The first time I went out to shoe his horses, I looked up from finishing a front foot right into the face of a giraffe who was calmly chewing the leaves off the tree by my head. I took a quick glance at the horse who, I was sure, would be at least surprised, if not panic-stricken, but I seemed to be the only one concerned. The horse wasn't even looking at the giraffe and the giraffe was pleasantly looking at me. I stepped away from the horse because I suspected he might have simply been day-dreaming and hadn't yet noticed the giraffe. I didn't want to be holding the leg of a horse who had just discovered a giraffe standing six feet away. But in a few moments, the horse casually looked at the giraffe and just as casually turned away to watch a cat walking across the field. I found out later that the giraffe was part of the next door "wild life" ranch that kept bizarre animals used in movies. The horse and giraffe were old acquaintances. The owner later told me that the horses were not so complacent the first time they saw the giraffe. They had noticed the "wild life" from about two acres distant and within seconds were at the farthest reach of their own 50 acres, from which vantage point they began to breathe again.

One of the delights about this ranch was the incredible coffee the Scottish customer's partner always served my apprentice and me. Within minutes of arriving, we would be handed a mug of strong black coffee on a tray with real cream and some cookies. The partner was always pleased to see us and seemed fascinated by our work. He usually sat and talked with us for an hour or so. The first time we met him, we had been working for about half an hour. We told him he probably didn't want to shake hands with us, considering what was all over them, but he did anyway. Then he said he would never wash his hands again.

We only worked with this customer for about two years before I moved to Oregon. I learned later that he had died of

AIDS. His death was a real loss to the world. He was as fine a person as I had ever known.

AIDS must be a terribly isolating kind of illness. I don't know much about it, but I would think an AIDS victim might lose a lot of lukewarm friends. In California we lived next door to a woman who had a son dying of AIDS. We knew nothing about it until after the son had died because no one ever came out of the house except to go get groceries or some other errand. We began to suspect something was wrong when we noticed their only visitors always arrived in a medical vehicle. After he died, the woman began to come out to work in her yard and we began to talk with her. She finally told us about her son and how they had moved to this house because they didn't want any neighbors to know about the disease. She said people weren't very nice to them when it was discovered that the son had AIDS. Neither of these two people had any support from friends or family. No one even knew they were there.

Culinary Aspects

People always ask me about feed for their horses. They worry about feed as much as they worry about their own diets. I usually tell them to ask their vet or go talk to the old guy at the feed store (any feed store will do), but over the years I've gotten enough information to be able to speak to this subject with some authority. I've learned that a chicken feed called "scratch" is a remarkable curative for crumbly hooves, that cider vinegar makes miraculous changes in arthritic horses, that horses behave better if the shoer arrives with a box of—God help us—sugar cubes, and that 50 percent of founder cases, a serious foot condition, occur on Christmas day because the owners run out to their ponies and horses with a gaily wrapped coffee can of sweet grain, an unaccustomed treat, which, if eaten in one sitting almost invariably ends in colic or founder, either of which can kill the animal.

I've also learned to be careful with my food words when I'm distracted by the job at hand. An example: I was trimming a new customer's horse and we were talking away in the usual manner when she asked me if I knew how to clean tarweed off the horse's muzzle and legs. Tarweed is a small bright green weed with little yellow flowers that horses enjoy eating. It puts out a sticky black tar that gets all over the

153

legs and faces of the horses. It's a real mess. Busy working on a hind foot, I admitted I had no answer for her, but suggested she go talk to the wise old home remedy expert at the feed store. "He'll probably give you some wacky recipe like kerosene and penis butter," I inattentively suggested. Horror struck, I murmured, "I mean 'peanut butter.'" I didn't look up. I didn't say another word. Neither did she. Without looking at each other the money was exchanged and I left. I've never heard from her since.

Getting back to food, one of the moderately bizarre but always present aspects of working with horses is the group of eager dogs who wait to eat the parings cut off the horse's feet. These parings are like giant toenails, only grosser. They're usually caked with urine, manure, and mud, and can generally be counted on to be incredibly smelly. Occasionally, they'll have a black, sticky, infectious, mucousy gunk, called, for some inexplicable reason, thrush. All dogs love this stuff. Knowing the shoeing routine, the barn dogs wait in eager anticipation for the first cut, sometimes catching it before it hits the ground. They fight over it, they slobber over it, they gulp it down, sometimes they throw it right back up, and wait for more. The fouler it is, the better they like it. I've often wondered what the horse must think, as it watches these carnivores fight desperately over parts of his body.

One riding stable where I worked had an Irish Wolfhound who loved hoof parings even more than most dogs. He was big enough to easily fight off other dogs so he could be first in line, but unfortunately for him, he was seriously allergic to the parings. The day he ate my contributions, he became deathly sick and had to have his stomach pumped, or, according to the vet, he would have died. Normally he was kept inside when shoers were on the premises, and they were all instructed to carry all parings away when they left. They were told not to put the parings in garbage cans, either, because the dog would tip over the cans and dig them out. But on the day I was there, he had inadvertently been left outside, and at that time I was unfamiliar with his history. I felt bad after hearing what had happened to him and how sick he had become. He recovered fully, but it must be difficult for a dog to live on a horse ranch and not be able to eat hoof parings on pain of death.

One day, at another ranch surrounded by the usual group of hungry dogs, I noticed the owner's four-year-old boy chewing something. I slowly put the horse's leg down, dropped my tools, and walked over to the boy. "What are you chewing?" I asked in my best conversational tone. He pulled a big chunk of hoof paring out of his mouth to show me. "The dogs like it, too," he said.

I had always thought about marketing this stuff to the pet shops as some sort of dog chewy. I didn't think poodle owners would feed horses' feet to their little pets, but I thought there were enough Doberman and Rottweiler owners out there to support my product. I knew that once the dogs tasted these treats, they would want more. But I couldn't figure out what to do about the dizzying stink—it seemed to be one of the stronger attractants for the dogs, but I couldn't imagine any human wanting to deal with it. Someone figured this out before me, however, and now you can find cows' hooves in all the pet stores. Made of the same substance as hoof parings, minus the stench, these sanitized little feet are a popular seller.

People and Their Animals

I'm always fascinated by what happens when animals and humans get together. People act strange around animals, even their own, and animals can really get bizarre around certain people. Horses, in particular, draw interesting behavior out of people. As an old cowboy once told me, "If it can happen with horses, it will." After all these years as a horseshoer, I can verify that with people *and* horses, if it can happen, it will.

Interspecies communication can be clear and productive at times; other times it's non-existent. How else can you explain the little lady who ignored the sign on the stall in the horsebarn that said "Dangerous Horse," and ignored the angrily flattened ears as she reached out to pet him—the little lady who sued the barn when the horse picked her up by the shoulder, pulled her into the stall, and trampled her? The horse communicated quite clearly with her. The lady was oblivious.

We are not always perceptive about what's going on in the head of an animal, even our own pets, but they can usually figure *us* out. What about the time your dog ate the two steaks off the barbecue? When you discovered it, you hid your rage, put a nice smile on your face, and with your kindest and most gentle voice you called him so you could beat hell out of him . . . and he wouldn't have any of it. No way

156

was he coming within reach. He saw right through you to
the real emotions inside. Animals have the power to do that.

Communications are distorted from time to time, but it's
usually the fault of the person, not the animal. I experienced
this kind of problem recently. My wife and I were driving in
the car with our big old Redbone Coon Hound in the back
seat. We stopped for lunch and left the dog in the car in front
of the window where we were eating a pork chop dinner.
Now sitting in the driver's seat, the dog watched each bite as
it moved from plate to mouth.

We should have let him out before this, but we forgot.
After we had eaten we went to put him on his leash for his
bathroom break. When we opened the door, he jumped out.
He is not supposed to do this. I panicked. We were parked
right beside a road where logging trucks roared by. The dog
had jumped out like this only once before, and I had really
yelled at him. He must wait until we tell him to get out, and
he knew this. I tried to control my alarm and calmly call him
over where I could get a grip on him. He knew something was
wrong, no matter how gentle my voice sounded, and he raced
around, running back and forth between the car and the road,
and barely avoided getting hit by two trucks purely by luck. He
didn't even know they were there. Eventually he noticed the
container of leftovers my wife put on the ground, decided he
wasn't in that much trouble, and came within reach. I hooked
him up to his leash and we all relaxed. The human/animal
communication system had been in a state of confusion for
awhile, but this time we all were lucky. No one was hurt.

I'm amazed at how some people relate to their animals
and house pets. I recently read some classified ads under

"Pets and Supplies" that made me more amazed. One ad to sell a cat read, "Big and Bold Redhead wants to be your one and only." I had to look at the heading a second time to make certain it was about a cat. I was embarrassed. Another cat ad informed the reader that "Flannery has a mischievous look on her face as she tries to figure out how to get the photographer to pet her." I didn't know anybody who would want a cat named "Flannery," and I didn't know anyone who would want a cat that put mischievous looks on its face to get petted.

Maddy, a "single girl seeking a permanent relationship" made me think I was in the "Personals" section, especially after I read that Maddy made "Great Muffins."

It's not that I don't like cats; I do like them. I've always had cats around. But I think of my cats as cats, not some cat/human cross that can cook and carry on a significant relationship.

The section on dogs wasn't much better. I read about Bambi, a year-old Pitbull who informed readers "I love everybody! I will steal your heart and I'm looking for someone who will keep me forever. Kisses and Hugs." A Pitbull named Bambi, for God's sake?

You can't blame the animals for this, but think how the owners who write this way about their pets act around the precious little furry ones, and what must those animals think about their owners? No wonder communications are bad.

Little furry animals aren't the only ones that can be spoiled by well-meaning folks. A nice lady called me to trim her horse in Northern California after I had been in the business about ten years. Over the telephone I asked her the usual question about the horse's behavior, and the lady said, "Oh, he's just a doll! He loves me to pieces. He even sticks his head in the kitchen to get cookies and goodies." I have no idea why warning lights didn't come on in my head. When I arrived at the lady's house, she, the horse, and several other people stood around to watch, another warning sign. I approached the horse to put my halter on him. He erupted. Up in the air he went, striking at me with his front feet. Not just once. Three times. Out of perversity, I kept trying to get the halter on, but there was no way to handle him. The lady was surprised. He had never acted that way before. She blamed it all on me. It didn't take me long to realize there was no way I was going to come out ahead in this situation. I suggested she might want to get the horse some training. She laughed, "It's just you that's the problem." OK. I know when it's time to leave. I've always wondered how long that horse's feet grew before she could get him trimmed.

If you think about it, you'll see that "bizarre" behavior in horses and other animals can often be blamed on people. Horses are basic and honest animals until they encounter humans. Then all kinds of strange things can happen. Horses read people accurately. A horse often knows what you are thinking or feeling, even if you don't, and will react to things in your mind that you may not even be aware of. An example of this is the time I let my five-year-old and three-year-old daughters take turns riding a gentle but very large paint horse I had just finished shoeing. The five-year-old went first. She was a rather boisterous child and sat up there kicking the horse. "Get up, Giddee up!" she shouted. All to no avail. The horse appeared completely unaware of her presence, and finally decided to lie down and roll. I yanked my daughter off just in time. (This is the same daughter who, as a two-year-old, was sitting in her high chair at dinner and noticed that the pineapple upside down cake was burned on the bottom. We were guests of one of my horse customers and none of the nine people paid any attention to her question, "Why is this cake burned?" Knowing what might be coming next, I tensed. She quietly looked around for a moment, and when she realized no one was going to answer her question, she shouted at the top of her lungs, "WHY IS THIS CAKE BURNED!?" Complete silence. This time they heard the question. I was too embarrassed to remember if she got an answer, but I suspect she did.) I pulled the horse back to his feet, and knowing that he was a safe horse, put my quiet but determined three-year-old on his back. She stared straight ahead and said, "Get up." He did. I later asked her how she had done that, and she said, "I wanted him to go and he was going to do it!" (This is the daughter who at age three came home from pre-school only to find some of her school art in the garbage under the sink. She took it out, looked at it, turned to her mother and me, and said, "All right. Who's the bastard who threw my art work in the garbage?")

If you pay attention when you're around animals, you might learn a thing or two. You might learn something about the animal, but you also might learn something about yourself. If a lot of people are standing around a horse and the horse is completely relaxed, and I walk up and it suddenly becomes tense or frightened, what is the problem? Most likely it's me. What can I learn from this? I may learn that I have brought the fear smell from my last horse and this horse can smell it. If that's the case, why was my last horse fearful? Was it my fault? Or, it may be that I am tense or fearful or angry, and the horse picks up on that. These kinds of questions have answers, and a careful observer can benefit from them. Animals aren't so good at human languages, but they understand emotion, tone of voice, and conscious or unconscious intent quite fluently.

Nicky, Miscellaneous Dumb Dogs, and Other Animals

Nicky, My Regular Horseshoeing Dog

For fourteen years, I had my wonderful Nicky, a Malamute-Husky-Wolf mix. I rescued her from a ranch in Sonoma County, California, where the owners had just loaded her up to take her to the pound for killing deer. "Ron will take her!" pleaded the tearful children. "Ron, you'll take her, won't you? Please take her!" What could I do? I took her. She was my closest friend for the next fourteen years.

Nicky knew horses. She respected them, but was never fearful of them. I often used her to chase a horse in a field when I had trouble catching the damn thing. She would run the horse until it was winded and I could walk up to it.

She was also my psychic bad-horse detector. After I had caught a new horse and tied it up, I would stand back and observe Nicky. If the horse was going to be well-behaved, Nicky would walk around it looking for hoof parings, and sometimes even walk under the horse. If the horse was likely to give me trouble, Nicky would keep a cautious distance and stay at least six feet away. I never could figure out how she knew.

One time I tied up an unfamiliar horse who stood there innocently. Everything looked all right to me, an easy job. Nicky kept her six-foot distance, but the horse didn't look like a problem to me. I picked up a foot and all hell broke loose. Nicky was right. This had to happen a couple more times before I became a believer. I eventually reached the stage when I would refuse to shoe a horse if Nicky did not approve. I could never bring myself to tell the customer I would not shoe her horse because my dog didn't like it. I just had to get really creative about my excuses.

Nicky could also detect ghosts . . . I think. I've heard that dogs can do this. One time my oldest daughter and I were sitting on the steps of a small cabin in the woods where we lived on a 2700-acre ranch in Northern California. It was in the fall, and the ground was covered with scattered oak leaves from the trees. We were sitting quietly when we heard the heavy breathing of a running dog off to our left. The sound came toward us, eventually crossed in front of us, and continued off into the woods on our right. We could see nothing, but we turned our heads in unison to track the sound. Nothing disturbed the leaves. My daughter and I looked at each other, and asked simultaneously, "What was that?" We both recognized the sound as heavy breathing from a running dog.

Later that evening, I took Nicky with me to the cabin where we quietly sat on the same steps. Suddenly, Nicky jumped up as if someone had hit her with a stick and ran with her tail between her legs to the house, about 200 yards away. I went after her, calmed her down, and took her back up to the cabin. We sat quietly for a few minutes. She suddenly leaped up once again, tail between her legs, and raced home. All my commands to come back went unheeded. Nicky had never shown fear of anything before this day.

We lived about 20 minutes from the nearest town, population 713, where six months later a local told me that an old prospector and his German Shepherd had lived (and died) near that same spot in the woods. The "ghost" dog.

As Nicky grew older, I had to lift her in and out of the truck. Her horse-chasing days were over. I thought I had lost her one time when I had her chase a horse in a large, closed arena, and the horse ended up chasing her. She was in danger of being run over. After I got her out of there, I never had her do that again.

Eventually, she could barely get up. She was suffering and seemed always in pain. I had to put her down. I took her to the vet's and held her while she received the injection that was to end her life. I had done this before with my other dogs, and I could tell when they had passed on. With Nicky, however, it wasn't quite the same. I carried her out and laid her in the back of my pickup to take her home and bury her. When I arrived home, my two younger girls ran out to see her. Nicky was lying on the tailgate, and the older girl, who was seven, noticed that she was still breathing. "It's a miracle," she shouted, running up and down the street, "She's alive! It's a miracle!"

I laid the dying Nicky out in the yard next to where I had dug her grave, and left her there until I knew she was truly gone. I put one of my horseshoeing hats over her head so I wouldn't be throwing dirt directly on her face, and buried her along with some old horseshoes.

The only thing she ever did that upset me was the time she ate my son's stool sample.

Lucy

I'm surprised at the life span of some dogs. It's hard to believe that some of them make it through puppyhood. I had a dog like that. I talked about this dog, Lucy, in the earlier part of this book where I insultingly called her "stupid." Read on. She was some kind of mixed mutt that my new girlfriend claimed to be half German Shepherd. I looked more like a German Shepherd than Lucy did.

Before I met the girl, she had kept Lucy in a huge wooden crate in front of her house where the dog barked throughout the entire day while the girl was at work, a fact verified by the neighbors on a daily basis. At night, Lucy slept in the living room where she deposited nightly the pile of shit that she had been saving up during the day. The girl asked me if I couldn't take Lucy on my daily horseshoeing rounds where she could provide companionship to me and my regular dog, Nicky. I agreed to give Lucy at least a trial run. I warned all concerned that Lucy, given her intelligence, would probably be stomped to death on her first outing, but that didn't seem to bother anybody. I hoped Nicky would be able to give Lucy some kind of education about being a horseshoeing dog before she was kicked to death.

Lucy's first day was memorable in that she didn't get killed at all. Upon arrival at the first ranch, she jumped out of the truck, ran up behind a horse and sniffed its hocks. The horse lifted that leg, as if to kick. Lucy backed off, and then trotted up and sniffed the hock once more. Once more, the horse lifted its foot in warning as if to kick and Lucy backed away and went off to eat an entire horse apple and roll in a dead skunk. At least she somehow had gotten the message that horses could be dangerous, and other than getting run over a few times, she was never seriously injured. That first day, my girlfriend seemed surprised that I returned Lucy in one piece. I wouldn't swear to it, but I thought I caught a brief look of disappointment in her eyes. She had probably already prepared the memorial service.

Lucy was not successful in getting herself killed by horses, but she did try to do herself in through others means. There was a new law where I worked in California that required dogs in the back of pickup trucks to be tied in. The county was tired of scraping flattened dog bodies off the roads, and rigidly enforced this new law. It took a real acrobatic dog to survive a fall out of a truck at speeds over 30 mph, although a horseshoeing friend told me how he watched in the rear view mirror as his dog sailed out the back of his truck on a sharp turn. The dog rolled about 20 feet, jumped up, and ran after the truck like he wanted to try that again. He was lucky.

When I heard about the new law, I immediately installed two chains to tie up the dogs. I was stopped several times by sheriffs over the next few weeks to make sure the dogs were, in fact, tied up. Lucy was comfortable with being tied in while the truck was in motion, but when we stopped for any length of time, she wanted out. On the first day she was tied in, I stopped for a cup of coffee and when I returned to the truck there was Lucy, hanging by her neck off the side of the truck with her hind toes just touching the ground. Standing on tiptoe she wagged her stupid tail at me as if she were proud of herself. I shortened the chains, of course, and never had that problem again. I know if I had not shortened the chains, Lucy would have continued to jump out at every stop until she succeeded in strangling herself. I never had that kind of trouble with Nicky.

Over the next few years, Lucy unsuccessfully tried various ways to do herself in, including eating two large bags of garbage and dumping several piles of the processed end product on the floor of the girlfriend's father's incredibly expensive and unfinished new wood dining room floor. I was not entirely surprised that the two bags of garbage didn't kill her, considering her digestive system, but I was surprised that the father didn't take her outside and shoot her. I don't think anyone would have objected.

There are lots of other Lucy stories, but besides being dumb, Lucy was boring, and these stories would probably be boring as well. I would be bored writing them. At least she wasn't a crotch sniffer.

German Shepherds, Ducks, Cats, and Wild Turkeys

A lot of dogs, like Lucy, seem to be determined to put themselves in harm's way, if not to actually get themselves killed. German Shepherds, in my estimation, lead this list. They just don't seem to understand that horses can hurt them. One customer had a German Shepherd that chased her horse on a daily basis and got kicked on a daily basis. He either had an incredible threshold for pain, a terrible memory, or no brain at all.

He used to cause me a lot of concern while shoeing that horse because he would walk under the horse as I worked on it. I couldn't keep him away, and the owner was never there to lock him up. The nervous horse always jerked around, agitated that he couldn't get a clear shot at the irritating dog, putting everybody in jeopardy, including the duck who was in love with that horse and attacked me whenever I got anywhere near him. The duck always followed us to where I would be working and did its utmost to get the horse to come back. I would have thought the dog would chase off the duck, but the dog was always too busy walking between the horse's legs in his usual efforts to get kicked or trampled. The dog would be irritating me and the horse on one side, and the duck would be squawking and hissing at me from the other side. I would chase after the duck with a rasp every few minutes, but I had no more luck keeping the duck away than I did the dog.

I thought I had taught this dog a serious lesson one time when his ear passed over the nail head just as I was hitting the nail. I, fortunately or unfortunately, was able to soften the blow just as it struck his ear. It still must have hurt like hell, but it discouraged the dog in no way. It could have been worse. I would hate to have had to tell the dog's owner that I had nailed her dog to the horse's foot.

That dog and that angry, jealous duck were there every time I shod that horse for the next five years. I finally moved away and didn't have to deal with them anymore.

Dogs and ducks aren't the only animals that walk under horses while you're working on them. Cats will do that, too. The difference is that dogs and ducks have a purpose in being under the horse; cats are just taking the shortest path to some place only they know about, but horses get just as agitated as they do when it's a dog or a duck. I've had as much trouble from cats around horses as I've had from dogs or any other animal. Kittens, however, don't seem to bother the horses. Three times I've watched a kitten run up the hind legs of a horse to sit on its back. In each of these cases I thought all hell was going to break loose, but it didn't. They were probably buddies, and the horse was used to it.

The biggest danger is what happens when you step on a cat while working on the horse. This invariably causes some kind of wreck. You get a shrieking cat and that's bad enough, but what disturbs the horse the most is when the shoer erupts and starts jumping around because he's stepped on a cat. It does have a way of breaking everybody's concentration.

Along with all the other problems they've caused me, cats have even added extra miles to my work travels. They will climb in the back of the truck and go to sleep hiding behind a nice smelly stack of old ropes and halters, and not even wake up when I load the equipment and drive off. Then when I get to the next place, I discover the cat and have to drive it back to where I got it, if I know where that is. One time a cat jumped from the anvil stand to my shoulder and walked across my back to get in the truck. They're usually not that obvious about it, but this was an unusual cat. I almost decided to keep him. What has always surprised me is my dogs never let on there was a cat sleeping next to them in the back of the truck. Maybe they planned to keep it themselves. These days, even if I haven't seen any cats around I'll still check the truck carefully before I leave a job.

Another entirely irrelevant story about cats is that rabbits can beat them up. My sister didn't believe this until she saw with her own eyes one of my rabbits chase a cat out of the yard. This is embarrassing to the cat. I watched a rabbit/cat standoff one time when the cat had stalked the rabbit and the rabbit stopped suddenly, turned around and faced the cat. They stood there facing each other until the cat started getting self-conscious trying to figure out how to get out of that fix and keep his dignity. The cat began to casually look around as if he had no further interest in that animal four inches in front of his face. The cat yawned, stretched a bit, and slowly turned his back on the rabbit, who suddenly jumped forward and bit the cat on his butt. The cat took off, all dignity left behind.

This kind of relationship puts the rabbit in a position of power over the cat, generally speaking, but when you throw another animal, a rat, into the equation, everything shifts. My kids had a bunch of gentle pet rats, and I wondered what would happen if a rat and a rabbit were to meet. So I put them both in an empty bathtub to find out. The rat immediately began to burrow into the rabbit's fur to bite him. The rabbit had absolutely no defense against a rat. I quickly grabbed the rat out of there and pondered the mystery of cats, rabbits, and rats. In our household, but perhaps not in too many others, the rabbit can beat up the cat, the cat can beat up the rat, and the rat can beat up the rabbit. My kids say it's a furry paper, rock, scissors game.

One of my customers had a ranch high up in the hills of Northern California that I used to enjoy driving to. The scenery was incredible. Herds of elk wandered through the woods, as did coyotes, foxes, and wild turkeys. One sunny day I drove up to shoe the three horses of Robert, the owner of the ranch. While parking my truck, I looked up and saw five huge turkeys racing across the yard toward me. Their feathers flopped around and they looked like a bunch of little old-fashioned ladies holding up their long skirts and running in full flight. I looked behind me to see if there was something that had attracted them, but no, it was me.

Having no idea what to expect, and a bit afraid they had decided to attack the next human they saw, I stood by my truck with one foot on the ground and one still in the truck. At this stage in my life, I had been shoeing horses for fifteen years and pride, ego, and self-esteem no longer played a part in my periodic decisions to run for my life, whether chased by a bear, a crazed goat, or a bunch of turkeys. I readied myself for flight.

The turkeys started throwing out their drag feathers to slow themselves down as they approached me and my truck, and finally stopped right in front of me. All five stood absolutely still, staring at me, unblinking. I waited for some indication of what they wanted, but none came. "Do I know you?" I asked. No response. Just as I was about to lose another staring contest with an animal, Robert showed up. "Those are wild turkeys," he said. I said, "Oh." He then told me their story.

They had appeared one day, wandering around on his property, and he had thrown them some bread scraps. They had been there ever since. When Robert told the fish and game guy about the arrival of the turkeys, the guy almost jumped at him, saying with vehemence, "Whatever you do, don't feed them! If you do, they'll never go away!" Well, there they were, and there they were going to stay. When they had run up to me, it was just to check out another sucker who might feed them.

After that day those turkeys loved my visits, and really got excited when I drove up because they knew there were going to be some hoof parings. Each time I started shoeing, the turkeys would sling aside their bread scraps that Robert fed them every day, and rush over to get the yummy fresh hoof parings. My dogs were a bit perplexed when this first happened, but they had seen just about everything, and wild turkeys just weren't that strange. Almost immediately the dogs jumped right in for their share. It was interesting to watch dogs and turkeys fighting over hoof parings. There were never any left over.

Those turkeys were there for over a year until some little bastard shot them.

More Dogs

Dogs can cause a lot of problems for ranch people. Especially sheep ranchers. In one area where I lived and worked in the mountains of Northern California, city folks, always with money, moved out to the country in droves. They brought their Fido's, their Fifi's, their King's, their Rex's with them, tied the appropriate red or blue neckerchief around the dogs' necks, and turned these household pets loose to run, to be free, as they thought dogs should be.

The dogs would get together in packs and in their bright country neckerchiefs chase and kill sheep. Cocker Spaniels, Poodles, German Shepherds, Pit Bulls, and Labrador Retrievers all gleefully chased, brought down, and ripped the throats out of hundreds of sheep on a daily basis. When confronted by irate sheep ranchers, the dog owners would deny that their Fido's, Fifi's, etc., would ever do anything like that. The dogs eventually accomplished what the wild pigs and coyotes had never been able to do: they drove the sheep ranchers out of business. This particular area in Northern California had been sheep country for generations, but no longer. The remaining sheep were sold and the ranchers replaced them with cattle. The terrain was definitely suited for sheep grazing, not cattle, and I don't know whether the shift to cattle eventually worked or not.

After the sheep had been moved out and the cattle brought in, television crews arrived at one ranch to film the Border Collies working the cattle. The dogs were held near the cameras, and at a given signal they were released and rushed out to work the cattle. Ready and eager, they ran out, looked at the cattle, looked around for the missing sheep, and finally just stood there bewildered. Whistled into action, they made a few feeble rushes at the cattle, who ignored them. I had to go back to work so I don't know how it all turned out. Given how intelligent Border Collies are, I'm sure they eventually got the hang of it.

One rancher, however, took the law into his own hands and shot a large German Shepherd in the act of attacking his sheep. He hung the dog's body from his fence on a main road. The sign tied around the dog's neck explained everything. Of course the public rose up in high dudgeon, demanding immediate and severe judgment on the rancher. The death penalty was suggested by more than one irate animal lover, the kind of person who was not in the position to have their livelihood torn from their grasps or food taken from their children's mouths by a dog looking for excitement. This was mostly a rural area, however, and the courts were sympathetic to the problems newly arrived city folks brought to long time established and respected ranchers. As far as I know, no one was ever prosecuted for shooting a dog caught in the act of killing livestock.

The county also decided to rule against city folks who would, for example, move in next door to an established pig farm, then take the farm to court because of the smell. The courts got completely fed up with this kind of city mind-set and refused to countenance further complaints of this sort.

The Dog Named Gus

A fellow horseshoer, Mike, had a mongrel dog named Gus, the same one who fell out of the truck before the leash laws, who always needed to be involved in something. He was not a dog to tolerate boredom. Gus lived on a large ranch where there were always lots of things to look at, chase, eat, or sniff, but Gus was so active that he often ran through these ranch dog opportunities early in the day and had a lot of time left on his hands. So he and Mike's horse invented a game. The horse always stood beside the fence that separated him from the rest of the ranch, and as a result of some un-spoken dog/horse communication, it was decided that Gus should also sit by the fence. The horse would stand with his head hanging over the fence, and Gus sat on the other side of the fence, just under the horse's head. Gus would lazily look around noticing the activities or lack of activities on the ranch. The horse, equally at ease, did the same. Ten or fifteen minutes would pass by as the two silently meditated on their surroundings. Then, at some point, the horse would suddenly seem to notice the dog who had been quietly sitting under his nose for a quarter of an hour or so. The horse would bend down to get a closer look and then look away for a few more minutes. The dog took no notice. The horse would repeat his evaluation of the dog under his nose maybe four or five more times and then bite Gus on his head. Gus would immediatcly jump up and bite the horse on the nose.

And thus it went: looking, biting, counter-biting . . . over and over for as much as an hour at a time. The game usually didn't begin until Gus had run out of other things to do, but it went on almost every day.

Even More Dog Stories

A Great Dane once escorted me up a driveway to the horse owner's house. That was early in my career when I didn't have sense enough to stay in the truck when there was no sign of any human around. Invariably, if the shoer drives onto a ranch or a private driveway, sees no one around and gets out of the truck to look for the customer . . . invariably, a dog or a bunch of dogs will come yapping out from somewhere. They're not usually aggressive, but sometimes they are. I no longer chance it. At a new place, I'll just sit in the truck until somebody shows up. Occasionally, I've sacrificed my dogs just to test the waters. I'll let them out of the truck and wait to see what happens. If there are ranch dogs around, they will usually ignore me and rush up to sniff around my dogs. There have been occasions, however, when my dogs chose not to be the guinea dogs, and refused to get out of the truck. Then we all waited for someone to show up.

Anyway, back to the Great Dane, which is really not a story at all; it's just an incident, an incident that hardly warrants the big lead up to it. What happened was simply that I got out of the truck and the Great Dane bounded down the driveway, took my left bicep in his jaws and gently marched me up to the porch where I was permitted to knock on the door. He waited further orders, I suppose, like whether he was to kill me or not. The owner verified my credentials and the dog left to go about his business.

A big, black Rhodesian Ridgeback hound provided me with my scariest dog moment. I was shoeing a couple of horses at a customer's house, when she had to leave. She told me to just put my coffee cup back in the kitchen when I was done. After putting the horses up, I took my cup in the house and headed for the kitchen sink. I was halfway between the door and the sink when I heard a nasty growl, and watched the Ridgeback rise up from the couch where he had been lying (the couch was facing away from me), and slowly advance on me. In front of the sink was a sack of garbage that had been scattered around the floor, the dog obviously being the culprit. I pointed at the garbage on the floor and sternly faced the dog. "Bad dog!" I accused. "You are a bad dog!" He stopped in his tracks, lowered his head and crept back to the couch. I left.

Other Kinds of Creatures

Domestic horses and cows aren't the only four-legged mammals that need work done on their feet. Sheep, goats, llamas, and baby mini horses also have hooves that sometimes need trimming. I'll discuss this group of animals because I have some limited experience in this area. There are other animals that should perhaps be included, like oxen who occasionally wear shoes, but I've no experience with them. Look it up in some other book.

Sheep and goats are easy. These animals have cloven hooves that are leather-like and softer than a horse's foot. Cloven feet double the shoer's work because there are two separate little identical parts to each foot, although "work" isn't exactly the right word. Most of the time it's a real pleasure to trim the feet of an animal that's smaller than you are. The feet will need trimming if the animal spends most of its time on soft ground. If the feet grow too long the animal could end up walking on its heels or the sides of its feet with useless, flappy parts curling out. If the feet of a sheep or goat grow too long, they will become twisted and distorted, throw the body off balance, and put a strain on the legs. A person would experience the same thing if they were to suddenly have a two-inch extension added to the toe of their shoe, or have the outside of the shoe one inch higher than the inside. The whole body would be affected as it tried to compensate for this change. If the terrain is cement, rock, or hard ground, cloven hoofed animals will wear down the excess growth just by walking around.

Hoof-trimming shears for sheep and goats look something like small tin snips and make the job fairly simple, but since I'm not a professional goat and sheep trimmer, I just use my horseshoeing nippers. Horseshoers get used to their tools and sometimes prefer them to more appropriate tools. I've used mine to work in the garden, to fix my truck, to make house repairs, to open cans, and to make furniture. I'm not great with carpenter tools, but I know how to get the most out of my horseshoeing tools. And I just recently repaired a faulty toilet seat with two handy-dandy three-pound shaping hammers.

My nippers are as long as the entire leg of the average sheep or goat, and can scare the owner when I walk up to their animal carrying something that looks more like a weapon than a tool. The difficult part is that you have to work the nippers with one hand, a trick in itself, because the other hand needs to be holding the animal's leg. Although goats and sheep are small, pleasant little creatures who never try to kill you, they are also little creatures who don't want their feet worked on. Yelling at them or threatening them will not get them to hold their legs still, so one hand has to hold the leg while the other hand does the trimming. Most of the time it's working with a moving target, so you have to be careful. Horseshoeing nippers could cut off half the foot if something went wrong. That little statement might cause a lot of sheep and goat owners to buy a pair of shears and do the job themselves.

I have no exciting adventures to describe with sheep and goats, except for the time I used my tin snips instead of my nippers, and cut myself. With one hand I tried to hold onto the leg of an energetic goat, and with the other hand I tried to trim a hoof with my large, unmanageable tin snips. I had thought they would be a more convenient tool than my nippers. With perfect timing the little goat jerked his foot and pulled my pinky finger into the line of fire just as I made the cut. I cut off a portion of that little finger and part of the nail. I like to work with these animals, however, partly because I enjoy feeling like I have some kind of control over them, but also because the work is easy, and the creatures are more entertaining than threatening. And they're little.

Llamas, however, are another story. I'm not going to risk offending the ever-growing population of llama owners by saying bad things about their animals. The fact is I don't know anything about their animals. I just know something about one llama named Pedro.

Pedro was a valuable and highly trained circus llama, and one day while I was shoeing some circus horses and ponies, Pedro's owner came up and asked me if I would trim his llama's feet. The only thing I knew about llamas was that their feet were similar to those of goats and sheep, but I said I would do Pedro when I was finished with the horse I was working on.

When I was ready, they brought Pedro over to me and explained that he was a bit temperamental. They said he would spit noxious fluids at me, so they put a sack over his head and snubbed him tightly up against the hitching rail. I wasn't sure what to expect, but began to relax after finding his front feet no harder to deal with than those of a large goat.

Things livened up a bit when I got to his hind legs. He kicked rapidly back and forth, making it hard for me to get ahold of the leg. As soon as I had it, however, I could hold on to it because he wasn't strong enough to jerk it out of my grasp. As I began to work on that foot, he suddenly lifted the other hind foot off the ground leaving me to hold up the entire hind end of the animal. That didn't overly concern me because he wasn't that heavy, and I could continue to work on him. What did concern me was when the leg I was working on suddenly seemed to come unjointed and ended up bent in a way that almost made me sick to my stomach. "I've broken the leg of this highly trained and expensive circus animal," I groaned to myself. "They're going to kill me." I lowered Pedro gently back to the ground and turned slowly to look at the owner who looked back at me. He stood there saying nothing. I needed to clarify the situation for him. "I think I've broken Pedro's leg," I confessed. The owner looked at me for a moment, and then laughed. "Pedro's double-jointed," the guy said. "He does that trick all the time."

I drew a deep breath, finished up Pedro, accepted my money, and went out and never did another llama.

I'm bringing mini horse babies into this section just because they are a completely different experience. Mini horses, often mistaken for ponies, are actually horses, just tiny, some not much bigger than a small goat. The babies are delightful, the kind you want to take home to keep in the living room. Most of my dogs have been bigger than these mini babies. Mini horse owners take exceptional care of their little charges, especially the babies, and are quite exacting in their expectations of horseshoers working with the animals. These owners watch the feet closely and will ask the shoer to begin trimming sooner than most horse owners will have their foals trimmed.

I've worked on a lot of these mostly pleasant little animals, adults and babies, but one case stands out in my memory. He was a very tiny baby, probably not much more than a month old, with feet about the size of a quarter. The owner said the baby needed a trim because one side had already started to grow faster than the other. I, of course, was still using my big nippers. Considering all the minis I worked with, I should have bought some smaller nippers . . . but I didn't. The owner, a very pleasant woman, and I were having some difficulty trying to figure out how I could get access to the tiny feet, when she came up with the perfect solution. She sat on the ground, picked up the baby, and held it in her lap with all four of its little legs sticking straight out in front. I got down on my knees but still couldn't comfortably work with the feet. The lady decided to sit up in a chair and hold the baby in her lap, and then I could get at the feet. It was like the lady was holding a tiny table in her lap with the four legs sticking straight out in front. A little pair of kindergarten scissors would probably have been a better tool than my nippers, but we got the job done. I think the baby enjoyed it. We used that system for about three trimmings until the baby was big enough to stand up to have it done.

The Donkey and the Spearcarrier

Two years into shoeing, I met Jose, a little donkey whose job was to pull a cart onto the San Francisco Opera's stage during the opera, *Pagliacci*. Canio, the lead character in this opera, traditionally first appears on the stage in a cart pulled by a donkey. In one performance in San Francisco, Mario Del Monaco sang the part of Canio. I was what is called a "supernumerary," often referred to as a "spearcarrier," and my part was mostly walking around on stage dressed as a peasant pretending to talk to other spearcarriers. We had a lot of rehearsals and Jose and I became pretty good friends off stage. No one else paid him any attention.

The week before opening night, the stage director decided to change the script to have Canio carried out on the shoulders of a man, rather than in the donkey cart. I was chosen to carry the 220-pound tenor on my shoulders (probably because I was the only one strong enough) and stand in center stage while he sang his opening aria. We rehearsed a few times, wobbling all over the stage, until through an interpreter, I got Mario to relax. Then I could hold him steady. During rehearsals, as we prepared for the entrance, Mario would climb on a platform, get up on my shoulders, and entertain himself by bouncing the two big padded drum sticks on my head in time with the opening music. Directly in front of me was a secondary clown character who carried a huge bass drum on his back. As we walked out onto the stage, Canio would beat the drum located right in front of my face.

Opening night was a great success as I stood on center stage holding Canio on my shoulders while I listened to his seemingly interminable opening aria. The reviewers praised the performance. One reviewer, however, had this to say: "The stage director's innovation of having Canio first appear on stage on the shoulders of a man, instead of in a donkey cart, added nothing to the performance and should be dropped." The next night, and all performances following, Canio appeared on stage in the cart pulled by the donkey. Jose and I remained friends.

Chickens

At one point in my life I decided that nailing metal shoes on large animals wasn't exciting enough, so I became a gentleman farmer. It wasn't much of a farm, just a corner lot in a suburban tract in Northern California, but to me it was everything. I started with chickens. A real farm has chickens. Wearing my brand-new leather farmer's gloves, I built a chicken coop out of old scrap lumber and chicken wire. It was magnificent—just like the how-to-build-a-chicken-coop book said. It even had little rooms (the book called them nests) where the chickens could lay their eggs, and where I could sneakily open a back door and snatch the eggs out from under the hens.

I threw handfuls of sawdust all over the bottom of their cage for them to walk on, and went out to get some chickens.

I bought some White Leghorns because the guy at the feed store told me that they were the ones that laid the eggs. I may rarely believe anything a horse owner tells me, but I always believe everything the guy at the feed store tells me. I put them all in the pen. It wasn't very exciting. They just looked at each other. Over the next few days, except for when my neighbor would throw garbage over the fence for them, their lives were pretty much hum-drum. I knew that cows who listened to music gave more milk, but I wasn't sure if entertainment would increase egg production. I felt like I should do something for them, so I introduced a different colored hen into the group. She was a Rhode Island Red, actually what is called a sex-link, but I don't think I can explain that. My children, who thought Dad had gone over the edge, but were rather entertained by it all, to my embarrassment named this newcomer Henny Cluck.

Henny Cluck was immediately rejected by the others, who to my horror, chased her all over the pen, pecking at her. There was no way they would let her near the food, so I had to wade through this agitated mob at least twice a day to feed her out of a special dish. This didn't make her any more popular, but at least it kept her alive.

It also made her into a pet chicken. Every time she saw me coming, she would rush through her current group of harassers and fly up against the gate where I was entering. After she started desperately trying to follow me out, I decided to give her her freedom. The first time I let her out, she followed me all the way across the yard and stood outside the sliding glass door staring forlornly through the glass at me after I went in the house. This became a pattern. It was disconcerting to sit down for breakfast and see a heartbroken chicken staring at you, watching every bite, eyes never blinking. So I let her in.

She now had the run of the yard *and* the house. We closed certain doors so she wouldn't leave her messes over the *entire* house, but generally she was free to come and go as she pleased. She would walk around on the dining room table picking at whatever interested her, and if unceremoniously pushed off the table, would strut, with dignity, into another room where, more times than not, she would crap on her favorite upholstered chair.

She was always overjoyed to see me when I came home, and would come flapping across the space between us and actually try to jump up on me, her bowels loosened with excitement. I knew you cured dogs of this jumping habit by stepping on their hind toes, but I didn't know what to do about a chicken. My eventual solution was to carry around a supply of Cheerios and put them down in front of her as soon as she ran up to me. Fickle, as you might expect a chicken to be, she always chose the Cheerios over me.

Of course this all led to some sort of Cheerios addiction. She would appear agitated until I gave her the Cheerios, then she would complacently ruffle her feathers and relax as much as a chicken under these circumstances could. Often, if I was sitting in a chair, she would hop up on my lap, eat her Cheerios (I was always prepared), and then sit there for a few minutes.

A few months later we moved to the in-laws' 2700-acre ranch in the hills of Northern California. I sold all the White Leghorns who had survived my attempts to cure them of their various illnesses, but took Henny Cluck with us. On the day of the move she rode loose in the cab of my truck accompanied by two dogs. They were in awe of her and left her quite alone. They even let her eat out of their bowls while they were eating. One time, Nicky, my smartest dog, figured she could avoid sharing her dinner with this damn chicken by picking up the bowl and carrying it across the yard. The problem with that solution was the food was falling out of the bowl as she carried it away. She found a good place to eat and set the bowl down. It was empty. Looking back where she had come from, Nicky watched Henny Cluck follow the trail of spilled dog food. She ate almost the entire bowl while Nicky watched, trying to figure out what had happened. I had to put Henny in the house—she was too full to eat any more, anyway—and give Nicky another bowl of food. I kept them separated during meal times from then on.

On the in-laws' ranch a strange cult who believed there was a spaceship from Uranus circling the skies waiting to pick them up had rented part of the property for their school. A few months later their rental check bounced and they disappeared into the night (on a spaceship?), and left us 400 young hens, each of which looked exactly like Henny. We let them wander around the property during the day, and locked them up in the barn at night. I was always amazed that there was no trouble between Henny and the others, although I occasionally was fearful that one of the 400 had usurped her position as First Chicken. I think the others recognized Henny's superior status and gave her space. She always went into her own coop at night.

When she died, I buried her in the front yard in a wooden box with a little jar of Cheerios.

Rabbits

Along with chickens, throughout this entire process, there were rabbits. A farm needs rabbits. This was all back in the protest days when people were giving up city jobs, putting red farmer's handkerchiefs on their dogs, and running off to the country to live off the land. I couldn't just run off, so I created my own little farm, complete with meat animals. This was where the rabbits came in.

My grandma in Tacoma always served rabbit for our big Sunday dinners, so I decided to carry on that fine tradition for my own family. The kids were ecstatic about the new rabbits, less so after hearing we were going to eat them, but I patiently explained the facts of middle-class America. Almost everybody eats meat and nobody takes responsibility for killing these creatures that we eat. We just buy a nice sanitized package of chicken or hamburger, I explained, and insensitively enjoy the meal, letting others take the rap for the butchering. That's not how it's going to be in this family, I promised. We were going to take responsibility. If we were going to eat meat, by God, we would be men (and girl) enough to kill it ourselves!

Of course the children were overjoyed. Now Dad is not only going to make them eat some cute furry little animal, he's going to make them kill it first. My four-year-old son momentarily found this interesting. "Oh, boy!" he said, but threatened by his six-year-old sister, chose her side rather than mine. They stood firmly together against my new program of responsible meat eating. The red-headed daughter gave me her stern look and said, "Daddy, that is mean!"

Once again stunned by the disloyalty of children, I altered course slightly. As soon as I chose the first sacrificial dinner, I knew I couldn't kill it in front of the children. I wasn't even sure I could kill it at all. I didn't even know how. Should I use a gun? A lethal injection? The book (always the book) said you hit it on the head with some kind of a club. I had a club. Then you cut off its head, feet, and tail, slice it open, pull out all the guts, being careful not to break the bladder, always full, or the green bile gland. A miscalculation in any of these acts could turn the entire nasty process into a real mess. I must have read those instructions 20 times.

Eventually, days or weeks later, I was ready. I bashed somebody's furry brains in, did all the messy stuff, and cut the corpse into nice little bite-sized pieces. It looked a lot like chicken. I started up the barbecue and threw those pieces on the grill. Cooked, they almost looked edible. I put the body parts on a plate and brought it to the dinner table where my innocent, albeit disloyal, children sat waiting for their evening meal. Here it is, I said. Your dinner. Rabbit. They looked at the plate, at me, at their wonderfully bemused mother, at each other, picked up a piece and ate it. I was dumbfounded. Totally unprepared for that kind of response.

I think I can state with certainty that they didn't learn a thing from this entire experience, but they did eat the rabbit. I'm not sure what I learned.

Two People and Three Cats

My twelve-year-old daughter and I drove up to spend a week visiting my cousin and his family in Canada one summer. This cousin and I, while we were growing up, got to visit on a regular basis. We were as close as brothers. As a boy, he was an interesting kind of nature freak and had a lot of animals, including ducks, around their small farm. We used to bury the ducks in sand with just their heads sticking out. My cousin was two years older than me, and knew all about his animals, so I never questioned this activity. He told me, "That's what they like," not "They like that," but specifically, "*That's* what they like." I told my wife this story years later. She had her doubts. But when she met him and we retold the story, he, true to form, shouted out, "That's what they liked!"

The cousins had a cute but strange young white female cat who was blind and partially deaf. She maneuvered around the house by rotating her head back and forth while emitting a curious sound between a quiet yowl and a grunt. My cousin said this worked for her like sonar. She could feel the sound vibrations bounce off furniture and that told her how close she was to bumping into something.

Shortly after we got there, my cousin and his family had to leave for a few hours and he warned us not to let the cat outside because she was in heat and he didn't want any cat babies, especially if they would be anything like the mother. We said we'd watch out for her. No sooner were the cousins out the door than we noticed a tough-looking tomcat sitting on the deck outside the kitchen smirking at us through the sliding glass door. He made what were probably some suggestive male cat sounds and started walking back and forth, never taking his eyes off the little white female cat on the other side of the glass who couldn't see him or hear him but obviously knew he was there. No problem, we said, and went in the other room to watch TV. A few minutes later I went back in the kitchen for something and there they were on the outside deck. I had no idea how she got out, but there she was, and there they were. I shoved the glass door open and rushed out yelling at them. The male cat eventually sauntered off and I directed the white cat back inside, although the damage was probably already done.

About the time I got the white cat inside, we heard a quiet meow and looked up to see a large yellow cat on top of the refrigerator. "How'd he get in here!?" we shouted at each other, and started yelling and whooshing at the refrigerator cat to get him off and out of the house before my cousins came home. He was not having any of it, and backed up tighter on the refrigerator where he appeared determined to remain. I finally got a broom and seriously assaulted him to get him out of the house and protect the questionable virtue of our white charge. It took some time, but I eventually got him down, chased him around the house and finally got him

out the door where he could join the rest of the neighborhood tomcats. My daughter and I each swore a pinky pledge
to say nothing about any of this to the cousins.

They came home soon after, and while eating dinner that
evening my cousin looked around and asked if we had seen
his yellow cat anywhere. Silence. "That's odd," he said. "He's
usually up on the refrigerator. He never goes outside." We
were enormously relieved when he showed up two days later,
but to this day we've said nothing about this to the cousins.
We have often wondered if the white cat had any kittens, but
we've never asked.

The Pig Who Thought He Could

A few years ago, some enterprising animal lover brought a Vietnamese miniature pot-bellied pig into this country. Being only a few weeks old, it was cute and everybody wanted one. More of the babies were brought in and people paid several hundred dollars for the little black charmers. Then they started to grow up. One of my Idaho horse customers, the finest person I've ever known, but who should have known better, bought two of them. If they had both been females or males, things would have eventually worked out all right, but they were a couple, a male and a female, entirely capable of reproducing themselves.

Before I get on with the story of Chester, let me describe what an adult Vietnamese miniature pot-bellied pig can look like. The female in this story, still alive, is so fat she can't move. She probably weighs eight or nine hundred pounds. If she were ever to raise her head, you wouldn't be able to see her eyes because they're buried in layers of fat. She probably couldn't stand up, even if she wanted to, because her belly is so huge that her feet wouldn't reach the ground. They'd probably just wiggle in the air like they were sticking out of her sides. Fortunately she is now so obese that the male can't figure out how to impregnate her, which is good, because she just squashes all her babies anyway. All, that is, except for Chester.

Chester is her remarkable son. He has a mission in life, the strength of which probably gave him the ability to avoid being squashed as a baby: Chester likes sex. Maybe sex isn't the right word, but it's close enough.

Chester learned much about life from his father who showed him around the farm. The two of them would walk side by side, checking everything out. He learned where the water was, where the best garbage was (on the back porch), and he learned about the other animals. He avoided the dogs, chased the cats, pushed the goats out of the way, ignored the chickens. He cared little for the brown horse with the runny nose, or the old retired race horse, or the stuffy mule—but he liked Patch, the big, good-looking palomino gelding. When I shoed Patch, Chester would either pace impatiently around the barn, or he would sit dejectedly in Patch's stall watching the procedure with a squinty eye, waiting for Patch to come back and take up where they left off.

The usual daily routine was for Chester and his dad to walk all over the farm, side by side, until bed-time. Then they would climb under the fence to sleep by Mama. Being active, Chester and his dad hadn't yet attained the wondrous girth of Mama, so they could still squeeze under the fence.

But Chester missed Patch during the long nights. Soon he started spending the nights with Patch instead of his family. He was growing up. He began to wander away from Dad during their daily rounds in order to spend more time with Patch. Much of this time was spent rubbing up against Patch's hind legs, often resulting in a kick that would roll Chester across the yard. But Chester persevered. He loved Patch and hoped things would change.

Patch, although probably not feeling the same passion as Chester, eventually came to be more accepting of his advances. But it was definitely an unrequited and unconsummated love affair. When Patch would lie down, Chester would try, in the best horse fashion, to mount him, but to no avail.

Chester did not entirely give up. Although a pig of determination, he was also a pig who knew when he was getting nowhere. He began to look around.

About this time the rancher bought some calves. His intention was to raise them to market size and sell them for a profit. Innocent to the ways of pigs, the calves began to relax when Chester was around them, even when he began to act strangely. Going at his own pace, and without losing his affection for Patch, Chester began his affairs with the calves. The strange, white sticky substance all over the backs of the half-dozen calves was a complete mystery to the rancher until the day he caught Chester in the act. Chester's owner had no idea what he should do about this.

But, as things go, one day a neighbor lady put her hand in the mess, smelled her fingers, and asked what in the world was that stuff. When she found out, she washed her hands steadily for a week.

Chester is slowing down these days. His dad has passed on and Chester spends more time in the mud with Mama. If he keeps on eating, he may soon be too fat to climb out under the fence. I have no idea what Patch or the calves would think about that.

I hear there is a place in the Midwest that takes in rejected Vietnamese miniature pot-bellied pigs. At last count there were 700 of them. I don't know whether these castoffs get pig therapy or are just left to wander around getting to know each other. I'm sure they're well cared for, but what would you do with 700 pot-bellied pigs?

More Pig Stories

Some of my best horse customers lived up in the hills of Northern California where horses were a way of life. We lived there, too. The houses and ranches were spread out and most people had plenty of room for horses used for working cattle and sheep, for pleasure riding, and for shows, fairs, and rodeos. It was horse country. It was also wild pig country. Almost everybody in the county had some kind of wild pig story where the storyteller had been chased through the woods and into the house, where pig and person raced around the house until the person jumped on top of the refrigerator in a final effort to save their skin. About half of these storytellers could show you the scars from the pig attack. The stories and scars all seemed to be authentic.

My stories aren't nearly as exciting. I seldom saw any wild pigs, but I saw signs of them. I raised a lot of rabbits that we either sold to pet shops or ate, and after slaughtering the ones for eating, I would throw the hides, guts, heads, and feet over a fence into the woods. By the following morning there would be no trace of any of this. The pigs came down and ate everything. Once I found a tail that had been overlooked, but everything else, skulls and all, had been eaten. I knew it was pigs and not vultures, because I could see the tracks. These pigs were also a nuisance to the sheep ranchers because the pigs became so bold as to start eating a birthing lamb before it had even fully emerged.

After we had lived there about a year, we saw our first "wild" pig. We had come home from a half day of shoeing and a half day of grocery shopping, and after closing the gate I noticed a pig rooting around in the front yard. I also noticed my brave dogs sitting quietly in the truck showing no interest in getting involved, even after my wife at the time had unchained them. My wife had not noticed the pig. When she did notice it she screamed and ran for the house, yelling at me to get in the house and to hell with the dogs. I just watched for awhile. The pig hadn't even seemed aware of all of us, not even looking up to see what all the screaming was about. He just kept tearing up the lawn and the flower garden looking for something good to eat. I eventually walked past him with the dogs who were looking everywhere but at the pig. "Pig? What pig?" We went in and ate dinner, and eventually went to bed. The pig was still there in the morning, looking quite refreshed after a good meal and a pleasant night's sleep.

I began to doubt how wild he actually was. He was colored like a domestic pig, but that didn't mean anything because most of the wild pigs had a variety of colors from mating with runaway domestic pigs. He barely took notice of me and the dogs as we loaded up the truck to go off to work. My wife decided to spend the day in the house.

When I came home that night, our neighbor, who was one of my horse customers and lived a few miles down the road, had roped this wild pig and was loading him in a pickup truck. My wife had tired of spending the day trapped in the house and had called the neighbor to come rescue her. He gave us a box of apples in exchange, which I didn't consider fair at all. I would rather have kept the pig who obviously was just an escapee from a local ranch and hadn't yet taken up with any of the uncivilized wild ones. That pig didn't make it through the week, and we didn't even get a pork chop.

The only other wild pig experience I had in this place was when my wife, her brother, and I went boar hunting. My brother-in-law and I each had a 30.06 with scopes, and my wife had a puny .22 rifle, also with scope. About an hour into the hills we spotted a boar up on a ridge about 400 yards away. My brother-in-law, who was the hunter, laid out the plan. He would flank the pig off to the left while we waited at the bottom of the hill, aiming at the animal. When we heard the first shot, we were to fire immediately. We waited and waited. Finally we heard the shot, saw it hit the boar, and watched him tumble down the hill toward us. We were on a little rise above the small gully that separated us from the hill the pig was rolling down.

We watched him fall into the gully below. He looked up at us with his beady eyes, struggled to his feet, and charged up the hill toward us. Into a big tree went my wife, shooting her tiny .22 shells in the general direction of the pig. "Get in the tree!" she shrieked, "and shoot that damned thing." I got in the tree but couldn't find the pig through the scope until he was almost up to our tree. By now he seemed really upset over the stinging .22 bullets and the shot that had toppled him. I finally got him in my sights and ended his struggle.

We dragged him back over a mile of rocky road. His hide was so tough the road didn't even tear his flesh. After butchering him, we put him in white butcher wrap and laid him to rest in our huge freezer chest out in the tack room, along with another wild pig, a half dozen packages of deer meat, twenty pounds of hamburger, about a dozen rabbits, and assorted other meats. We were set for the winter.

The problem was that the freezer was on the same outlet as the overhead light, and both were turned on and off by the light switch beside the door. At some point in the next few weeks, someone (I think it was my father-in-law) had come in and turned off the light switch that we always kept on. That turned off the freezer. When I went out to get a couple of rabbits and some hamburger for a birthday barbecue with a group of friends, the stench hit me like a wet gunny sack. I held my nose and looked in the freezer. Not only was there no indication that anything had ever been frozen, there was heat rising up off the packages of rotting meat.

Instead of a birthday barbecue that night we all drove into town for Mexican food. Instead of playing party games, we all went out to the tack room and took turns heaving the packages of rotten meat out the tack room door.

The next morning I counted 27 vultures unwrapping white butcher paper packages, oohing and aahing over the contents, and eating everything but the paper and some ribs. It took them about two hours.

Youth Rodeo

Cowboys and Cowgirls don't just rise up completely formed off of some cattle ranch, and although some people might disagree, most are not born, they are made. A lot of these youngsters start up on ranches and farms, but the proving grounds for many is the Youth Rodeo. The ages of the participants range from two to nineteen.

Youth rodeo in my part of the Northwest usually has four divisions: Pre-Pee Wee (ages 2 to 5), Pee Wee (ages 6 to 10), Junior (ages 11 to 13), and Senior (ages 14 to 19). For several years I've volunteered at these rodeos in what is called the "stripping chutes," where the lassoes are taken off the steers and calves after their event and the animals are driven into pens, and I am humbled and astonished at the courage and talent of these young boys and girls.

The rodeo grounds where youth rodeos are held are the same grounds used by professional rodeos, and the people and the scenery look much the same. The crowds are much smaller, however, made up mostly of family members. You'll see the same competitors walking around wearing big earned silver buckles large as saucers, but these will mostly be on children . . . little five- and six-year-old boys and girls, cocky young eight-year-olds, serious and competent eighteen- and nineteen-year-olds. You'll hear country music playing in the background both before and during the rodeo. You'll see cowdog puppies on horses' lead ropes everywhere, and may hear an opening prayer that doesn't ask for help to win, but to do their best and avoid injury. There will often be a couple of hardy-looking seven-year-old boys or girls wearing fancy cowboy shirts embroidered with the names of local sponsors, and during the opening ceremonies you'll see tiny little three- and four-year-olds proudly racing their ponies all around the arena, hats blowing off all over, none getting stepped on by horses.

Looking at the Day Sheet that lists the competitors and their events, you'll frequently find good old Western names like Cody, Wyatt, Clay, Jake, Cole, Jessica, Emily, Dakota, Blake, Cheyenne, Justin, Shawnee, Lacy, Baylee, and Cassidy.

Before the rodeo gets underway you might hear the announcer warning the volunteers in the arena about the rodeo dress code: cowboy hats, boots, jeans, long-sleeved shirts, no tattoos showing. Very infrequently you'll see what I saw recently: a blond yuppy lady in the stands wearing shorts, tank top, and sandals, completely ignoring the rodeo and bothering the people around her by talking loudly on a cell phone about property analysis.

The Rodeo Queen and her Court race out during the opening ceremonies. The ages of the Queen and her Court at the last youth rodeo I attended were 13, 13, and 8. The criteria for selection were: Personality and Communication Skill, 40 percent; Appearance of the girl and the horse, 20 percent; and Riding Ability, 40 percent.

And if you're lucky like me, you'll see a tiny cowboy in cowboy hat, boots, jeans, shirt, chaps, and a pacifier in his mouth as he tries to lasso his dog with a rope.

I talked with a young Pre-Pee Wee competitor and her mother prior to the opening ceremonies of one local rodeo, interested to get the child's thoughts on rodeo and life in general. The girl was decked out in complete cowgirl attire—hat, boots, chaps, Wrangler jeans, and western shirt—but she wasn't much for talking. When I asked her how old she was, she held up three fingers. She said her name was Hayley, and her pony's name was Ringo. Beyond that she didn't have more to say, so her mother answered for her. "Where did you get that great big buckle?" I asked. Mother said it was a "participation" buckle from the previous year when Hayley, at the age of two, had participated in 51 percent of the year's eight rodeos. Hayley smiled proudly. Her events were Barrel Racing where three large metal drums are placed in triangle formation and the rider directs the horse around those barrels in the correct pattern, and Flag Racing where the rider races down to a barrel that has a coffee can on top with a flag sticking out of it, and the object is to get the horse close enough to the barrel to grab the flag and race back across the finish line. These are timed events. In Hayley's case, her performance is restricted by her mother's speed and endurance because her mother leads Ringo around by his lead rope in both of these events. Hayley seemed a little disturbed by this idea of being led around by her mother. I got the impression that Hayley thought she could probably do it faster on her own. Next year, Mom promised. As I was leaving them, Hayley told me she liked Ringo a lot.

The Pre-Pee Wees also have an event called Goat Tying where the little cowboy or cowgirl rides across the arena to where a baby goat is tethered to a post and held by an adult. The little rider tries to ride up as close as possible to the goat, jumps off the horse and runs over to tie a ribbon on the goat's tail. Several factors enter into this seemingly simple procedure. Since the competitors are between the ages of two and five, they are usually quite small, some even tiny. This presents a problem getting off the horse. Getting on the horse is easy, the parent puts the child up there. At the other end of the ride, however, there is no parent. What usually happens in this event is the child is helped aboard the horse or pony, races down to the goat, and falls off the horse or pony like a sack of potatoes into the soft dirt. There is nothing to be done about this. The distance from the back of the horse or pony to the ground is way too far for a gracious descent.

The next problem is the process of actually tying a ribbon to the tail of the baby goat. The goat isn't the problem for the Pre-Pee Wees; the ribbon is the problem. It is often carried in the child's mouth where it is to be retrieved for the purpose of tying it to the tail. Occasionally, however, in the excitement of the competition the ribbon falls out of the competitor's mouth and is lost somewhere in the dirt. Searching for it is useless because the limited amount of time (a good idea) allowed for the event will usually end before the ribbon can be found. Assuming, however, that the child survives the drop off the horse and is still holding the ribbon, the next difficulty may be that the child isn't very good at tying knots. This is serious. Despite hours of practice at home, the child in the throes of competition often completely forgets the steps required in tying a knot. All the shouts of encouragement in the world won't help, and verbal instruction under those circumstances is useless. Regardless of what happens at the ribbon tying stage, the child is eventually told to throw his or her hands up in the air, the victory signal indicating that the job is complete. Sometimes the ribbon is actually tied on the tail, other times it ends up just lying on the goat's butt, but the child is still a winner.

During one of these Pre-Pee Wee goat-tying events, two large bulls broke out of the chutes into the arena where the goat tying was going on. They were eventually chased back in by one of the clowns and some riders on horseback. The adults handling the goats were petrified; the little competitors didn't even notice, throwing their hands up in the air triumphantly when they were finished.

The idea of everybody coming out a winner is a good concept that pervades the youth rodeos that I've seen over the years. Everyone is a winner. Even the little girl who fell off her horse during the Grand Entry was generously applauded as her dad carried her out the arena. Her little cowdog was the first to run into the arena to check her out. She was crying, but she still waved to the spectators. The little six-year-old boy or girl who gets thrown off during a bucking event almost before the animal leaves the chute is wildly applauded by the spectators. Older competitors, who have been there and know what courage it takes to even climb on the back of one of these animals, sincerely congratulate the small competitors for a good try.

The Pee Wee division (six to ten years) is where the going starts to gets rough. These youngsters have barrel racing like the Pre-Pee Wees, and an advanced form of goat tying where a full grown goat is tethered on a ten-foot rope but not held by an adult, and with no mother's help, and the rider has to get off the horse and catch the goat to complete the tie. But the rest of their events require even more skill and courage, like the Bareback Riding and the Bull Riding.

If the rider is six or seven years old, and small, he or she will be given a bucking pony to try to ride. Older boys and girls in this age group will often ride actual bucking horses chosen for their bucking ability in combination with a limited aggressiveness. There is no question that this is a seriously dangerous event, but precautions are taken by using gentler, older horses and putting helmets and protective vests on the little riders. These protective devices are often used by the Senior riders, as well.

In the Bull Riding event for the six- and seven-year-olds, the "bull" is often a steer and sometimes even a cow. The arena announcer doesn't point that out, however, and when the little rider breaks out of the chute, the announcer will often say, "That's a pretty wild looking bull our rider has drawn!" even though the "bull" has an udder. But the danger of getting thrown and stepped on or kicked is always present and potentially serious. The older eight- to ten-year-olds will probably get a bull, smaller perhaps and with less dangerous horns, or maybe no horns, but no less threatening to life and limb. In the first ride in a recent rodeo, an eight-year-old boy had his arm broken when the small bull threw him and stepped directly on the arm. He was hurt, but that boy had bravely started his career as a rodeo cowboy.

There is always drama in the chutes when the bucking horses and bulls are brought in and loaded into the individual chutes. Experienced riders and fellow competitors hover around each chute helping the rider put his or her gear on the animal and climb aboard. There's a lot of support. "You can do it, Cowboy (or Cowgirl)! Lean back, hang on. You can do it!" are the kinds of encouragement given everyone. I doubt that much of it is actually heard, but the little riders know it's there and that a lot of people are rooting for them.

Surprisingly, few of these young riders change their minds and back out at the last minute, but if they do, there is no stigma attached to what is probably good judgment kicking in. Recently, I watched a dark-haired Pee Wee boy named William who was planning to ride in both the Bareback and Bull Riding events. He had on his vest and helmet with the protective face mask, but he was having second thoughts about getting on that pony for the Bareback event. I couldn't blame him. The pony jumped, kicked, and raised all kinds of hell in the chute as they tried to get the gear on him. The boy watched all this and listened to his mother who was telling him he could do it, but it would be OK if he chose not to. He was crying and his mother was hugging him. Older cowboys trying to hold the pony told him he could do it, but when he finally said he wasn't going to, they said maybe next time, and some of them told him about the times they also had been too afraid to ride. There was nothing but support and understanding and praise. After all, how many people would have gotten as far as that boy had? While watching a hardened cowboy hugging his crying eight-year-old boy who had been thrown by a bull, I compared this support with what I had seen of some Little League fathers and mothers screeching at their child for striking out or dropping a fly ball in a baseball game.

I talked to William, the little cowboy, and his mother later. When I asked him how old he was, he held up five fingers, which was incorrect, since he had just turned six. He wasn't embarrassed or ashamed in any way about dropping out of that ride. "That pony was bigger than me," he said. (When they turned the pony out into the arena, it took two cowboys on horseback ten minutes to get him back into one of the holding pens.) William ran off to play with some friends, one of whom told me, "He has to ride the bull, because he swore he would. Now he has to!" Later, I saw William and his friends, all dressed in their cowboy outfits, down on their knees playing with trucks in the stands.

Later in the afternoon of this same day, William arrived at the bucking chutes with his helmet and protective vest for the Pee Wee Bull Riding event, but the same scenario developed. He took one look at his "bull" and chose common sense over risking his neck. I guess the universe can probably tolerate a broken "swear" from a six-year-old cowboy.

There are six events for these six to ten-year-old Pee Wees: Bareback Riding, Bull Riding, Breakaway Roping, Poles, Goat Tying, and Barrel Racing. The Poles event requires the horse and rider to weave through a series of poles set up in a straight line. For most riders the object is speed. For some of the younger ones, the object is to get through the course. The older Pee Wees are usually quite focused. The younger ones are more prone to distraction. Generally speaking, if at least one of the two participants—horse or rider—is focused, things go fairly well. For example: a concentrating six- or seven-year-old rider may keep a distracted horse or pony on course, and, on the other hand, a well-trained animal can run the course correctly even though the rider is cheerfully waving at friends and family in the stands. If, however, you have an untrained horse and an unfocused rider, you may see them drift happily all over the arena, oblivious to shouts from family, friends, and judges. At least they're having a good time.

In Breakaway Roping, the rider on horseback tries to rope a running calf, and if successful, the rope will break free from the rider's saddle and the calf will run off with the rope around his neck or whatever part the little roper has managed to catch. The kids in this event are usually quite proficient and always determined. Hating to miss their throw, these riders often wait until they've got a really good shot. Sometimes the roper and calf end up racing all over the arena, running into fences, chasing each other in tight circles, but these little cowboys and cowgirls usually make a successful throw more often than not. One time I saw a tiny little roper fall off her very large horse, calmly walk right under him, and determinedly pull herself back up into the saddle.

In the background you'll frequently hear the mother cows bawling for their babies who are participants in this event.

The 11- to 13-year-old Juniors have the same events as the Pee Wees, with the addition of the Calf Tying event. This does not require catching the calf. It is already tethered in the middle of the arena. The youth rides up on a horse, drops off, runs to the calf, throws it to the ground, and ties three of its legs together. This can be a struggle, especially for the smaller competitors, occasionally calling for innovative methods. At one youth rodeo, a smaller 11-year-old boy had trouble throwing his calf, and ended up in a full-blown wrestling match. Sometimes the boy was on top, sometimes the calf. They both finally collapsed in a heap with the boy lying flat across the calf while trying desperately to catch a leg to tie his rope to. From where I was watching, it looked like the boy had two of the calf's legs and one of his own in the tie, but I'm not sure. The boy had a big grin on his face when he finally got up.

The Senior Division calls for much greater skill and courage, especially in the three events of Bull Riding, Bareback Riding, and Saddle Bronc Riding. The animals in these events are full-sized and not to be trifled with. They do not take kindly to someone trying to ride on their backs. The bulls will frequently charge a thrown rider, hopefully turned aside by the rodeo clown bull fighters who are intent and professional, particularly when the Seniors are competing. Accidents can and do occur much more often in the Senior riding events, but by the time these young people have reached the Senior division, they usually have ten- or twelve-years' experience and know the risks they are taking. Sam, a quiet young 19-year-old, after successfully riding a particularly nasty bull, told me he had been rodeoing for 16 years. He plans to ride in the PRCA (Professional Rodeo Cowboys' Association) next year.

Chute Dogging is a unique event for Seniors where the boy climbs right inside the chute with a steer, holds on to the horns, and tries to throw the steer to the ground once the gate is opened. Larger and stronger boys usually complete the throw within the time limits, but the smaller competitors face a more difficult task, often being dragged across the arena through the mud and the dirt, only to walk all the way back with huge grins on their faces.

No matter the age, and win or lose, most of these youth rodeo boys and girls will be back next year. Many of the older Senior division boys and girls will go on to compete in professional rodeo, their years with the youth rodeo having prepared them well. But they'll also be back to help the younger kids in next year's youth rodeo.

I need to mention one more event: Mutton Busting. Primarily for younger, mostly inexperienced boys and girls, this event ranks high in audience appreciation. As many as 15 wooly sheep will be dragged and bullied by adults into a semblance of a line, while the youngsters are planted on the animals' backs. At the whistle, the children hang on for dear life, their hands plunged deeply into the wool, and off they go. Everywhere. The arena is filled with racing wooly bodies and little kids hanging on, slipping off to the sides, eventually falling in the dirt. The last child to hit the dirt is the winner. Sometimes this event is over almost as soon as it has started, but every now and then, two or three little competitors refuse to be thrown. Hanging on with arms around the sheep necks or with little fists dug deeply into the wool, these children are not going to let go. Around and around they scramble. Usually there is a final winner, but every now and then a tie has to be called so the rest of the rodeo can get started. This is an event I would be willing to encourage my grandchildren to enter.

The best summary I can give of youth rodeo is that it's set up so that everyone learns something about life and rodeo . . . and everyone comes out a winner.

The Youngest Cowboy

One of my daughters teaches at an expensive private daycare/grade school facility and she tells me stories about some of the younger students, the four- and five-year-olds. Some of them seem to have quite a time of it. If they don't get their way, or some other kid takes their toy, they throw all kinds of fits. They cry, scream, throw themselves on the floor, hit everyone around them, run out of the building. The choices are unlimited. The teachers then have to reach into the bag of tricks learned in their child behavior classes at college and come up with some method to quell the outburst without doing any emotional or physical damage to the kid. If they touch the kid they will be sued, of course, by irate parents who do not believe in spanking their children or doing anything else that might traumatize them. These parents probably allocate 10 percent of their income to buy child behavior books and take parenting classes in order to raise the perfectly adjusted child. No physical punishment, no criticism, no loud voices. The child must be respected and allowed to participate in its own development. "I understand you are angry at your little sister, but can you think of a different way to show your displeasure? Setting her hair on fire is not really fair to her. Would you like to tell us how you feel about that?" There are hundreds of themes like this.

Whenever I hear these horror stories, I think about some horse customers I had in the hills of Mendocino County, California. The family raised both sheep and cattle on their 2,000-acre ranch, and all the work was done by the man, the wife, the hired hand, the dogs, and Jimmy, the four-year-old boy. They had a string of eight horses that I shod every eight weeks, always putting heel calks on them so they wouldn't slip on the steep hills of the ranch. The calks were like football cleats designed for maximum traction.

This family was an absolute joy to be around. They always laid another place for me at the lunch table where we ate their own grass-fed beef, lamb, or pork, and garden vegetables, mashed potatoes and gravy, cornbread, homemade apple or berry pie, milk, and gallons of good strong coffee. The conversation was always stimulating and relaxing at the same time. We talked about everything from cattle and horse diseases to books we had read, to politics, to the meaning of life. None of the family was formally educated, but they had an interest in everything around them. They were thoughtful and open thinkers and gave serious consideration and respect to everybody else's opinion. Jimmy mostly listened, but he was completely at home sitting with the adults and eating quietly with good manners, occasionally asking a question or contributing something to the conversation. Both his questions and his contributions were given the full attention of everyone else, the same respect that was given to my questions and contributions. No one was condescending to him in any way and he behaved as you might expect someone to behave whose opinions were always respected and who was never condescended to. If he was in error on some issue, the error was discussed. If I was in error on some issue, that also was discussed. There was always a lot of joking and laughter that was never petty or mean. I looked forward to spending time with these people every eight weeks when the horses were due for shoeing.

I titled this section, "The Youngest Cowboy" because Jimmy, the little four-year-old was, in fact, a working cowboy. When it was time to move cattle or sheep, all hands joined in. Father, mother, hired hand, dogs, and Jimmy. Everyone had a specific job to do, a particular section to ride. If a bunch of steers broke loose from the drive, the nearest person on horse went after them. Jimmy usually rode drag, a responsible position bringing up the rear, but he was always ready to ride wherever he was needed. Being so small on a large horse, he occasionally fell off. But he didn't throw any fits and it took a pretty bad spill to make him cry. His injuries were never downplayed. No one ever told him, "Stop crying! You aren't hurt," or "Cowboys don't cry," or "Don't be a sissy." Likewise, no one ever over-coddled him. His problems and his injuries were treated the same as anyone else's. After all, they had a lot of livestock and not a very big crew. All hands needed to be healthy and happy. All hands were needed.

I moved away from that area after a couple of years, and about the time I left, Jimmy was scheduled to enter the first grade down in the valley school. I have often wondered how he would react to that experience. On that first day, would he be confused, upset? Probably puzzled. He might find a few other small ranch hands in his class, but what would he think of those little classmates who might be crying for their mommies, or hiding under chairs, or throwing fits? Here he was, a working cowboy thrown in with that bunch. Heck sakes, they probably wouldn't even be any good at all on a cattle drive.

I suppose some might say this little boy was denied his childhood. Where were all his toys, his stuffed animals, his little playmates, and what about TV? He never even got to watch *Sesame Street*. Well, he did have a few toys and stuffed animals, but according to his parents he much preferred the working life. Granted, he didn't have the company of children his own age, but he certainly learned socializing skills under exceptionally healthy circumstances. His concept of self was solid. He was as comfortable in my presence, a stranger, as he was with his own family. According to his mother, he was always relaxed in the company of new people or visitors, looking forward to what they might talk about. A curious, mature little boy, always respected, loved, and nurtured, he was becoming a child who enjoyed life and accepted all things whether they went his way or not. He learned from his mistakes. I'd say that was a pretty good childhood, probably better than that experienced by a lot of the children in my daughter's class.

Graduation

I've finally received my doctorate from the University of Oregon. It's taken me 12 years to develop a Celtic Studies major for colleges and universities, partly due to procrastination and discouragement, partly due to administrative confusion. The only connection this short section has with horseshoeing is that horseshoeing kept me in the real world that the Ph.D. program kept trying to drag me out of. I'm just now finding myself able to turn on my computer without my heart pounding in anticipation of the next administrative botch or the revelation of a deadline I had failed to meet. I am beginning to be able to look at my university's logo on passing cars without getting sweaty palms. I can drink my coffee out of my university logo mug, while wearing a U of O baseball cap.

I'm not going to describe the horror of this educational experience or the campus politics and other things often associated with university departments. I'm just going to give thanks to my advisor, Dr. Diane Dunlap, and all those horses who helped me through the process. My old horseshoer buddy, Gary, used to give me a lot of grief because he said I always thought too much, mostly about the enormous and unsolvable problems in my life. "You need to get under more horses," he always told me. "You think too much. Get under more horses." Thanks, Gary. That advice, although not always followed, has done a lot to keep me going over the years. Thank you, horses. Thank you, Gary.

At the university graduation, I wore my 35-year-old cowboy hat (with gold tassel, of course) instead of the doctoral tam. They put me on TV.

Dad

I'm sitting here with my Dad in the California convalescent hospital where he is spending the last days of his life. This is the man who had been a college All-American and professional football hero, was an Olympic-class track man, and had been the sparring partner for Freddy Steele, the middleweight boxing champion of the world. This is the dynamic, strong-minded giant who dominated my early years and who, in some ways, still does. Now he sits in a wheelchair, hooked up to a feeding tube inserted in a hole they cut in his stomach because he can't swallow. He makes choking noises. He's not wearing his teeth because they hurt, and his mouth is shriveled up into what you might expect on the face of a 91-year-old man.

It takes enormous effort for him to move any part of his body, and he clutches a rolled- up towel they put in each of his immobile hands. I have no idea why. They've put one of his old baseball caps on his head, probably to make him look more like a human being, but it's on crooked and I feel stupid trying to straighten it out. Will that make him look more alive? It looks ridiculous.

I can't imagine what it must be like to be unable to move. If I sit in one spot without moving for any length of time,

I start to feel uncomfortable and I shift my weight around. He can't even do that. If he itches, he can't scratch; if he has a cramp or any kind of pain, he can do nothing but suffer it. He can't even tell anyone what's wrong. His skin will tear like some kind of parchment if he is left in one position too long. He has massive bruises all over his arms. The nurses tell me it is from being immobile. It pains me enormously to see him groan and try to move, his face contorted, and I don't know how to help.

I've just read a chapter out of this book to him and he fell asleep in the middle of it. I haven't seen him for several months since he was moved to California, and I've looked forward to seeing the pride in his face as he listened to the book his son was writing. When he fell asleep I thought it was because my writing was no good. His hold on me is still strong.

A week ago my dad got pneumonia and my sisters and I decided we would let him go that way. They say that pneumonia is the old person's friend because it's a relatively easy death, so we told the medical staff not to treat the pneumonia, but just give him medication for pain—as we braced ourselves for the end. He's just a prisoner in his own body and we know he would have hated being like this. Two days ago he cured himself. The pneumonia is gone. The nursing staff was jubilant, but why? What kind of life is this for him? There's no dignity in any of this.

I guess in the big picture there's meaning to it all. Obviously he's not ready to leave, whatever the reason. My sisters and I thought maybe our mother, who died two years ago, is telling him to hang on a little longer so she can have a few more days of peace before he goes to join her. She loved him dearly, but in her last days he was driving her crazy. She never lost any of her mental faculties and had to use them all to keep Daddy from doing things like setting a newspaper on a hot stove and burning down the house . . . or worse. A few days after she died, my father came out of his bedroom at 3:00 a.m. and woke up the sweet little old devout lady who was caretaking him. "Let's have a sex party," he said. She got him back into his bed and quit the next day. He didn't remember saying that.

Mom and Daddy had a strong and loving relationship. They were so close to each other that sometimes us kids felt left out. Their relationship got more interesting as they grew older and Daddy got more set in his ways. Mom was always patient and gentle, but with a sharp humorous mind that no one wanted to challenge. Except Daddy. He got more curmudgeonly as the years went on, sorely testing Mom's patience.

To help them celebrate their 60th anniversary, my two sisters and I treated them to a weekend at an upscale beachside resort on the Oregon coast. Mom was excited. Daddy didn't want to go.

One of my sisters drove them to the resort and my wife and I, and younger girls, ages six and nine, arrived shortly after to have dinner with them. Daddy started up the minute we got to their room. "Good. You're here," he grumbled. "Now you can drive us home." Mom patiently explained to him that they were there for a wonderful vacation, and for my dad to heal from the infected scratches he got from teasing the cat. Back and forth went this argument, with Daddy getting more and more determined to go home, his voice getting louder and louder. Finally Mom said, "Red, we are going to stay here all week and enjoy each other's company!" She paused . . . and then burst out laughing. Daddy laughed too. Then he farted. "It slipped while I was getting a new hold on it," he explained.

As we left for dinner, I took the room key because I knew Daddy would lose it. He looked at me and said, "Give me the g.d. key!" I decided to become the adult and for the first time in my life I launched into a lecture to my own father. I told him he had spent his entire life caring for others, and now it was time for him to step back, relax, and let others care for him. On and on I went. It was a great speech. Everyone, including Daddy, stood quietly and heard the whole thing out.

Feeling really proud of myself, I headed for the restaurant, the others quietly following. A few steps later I heard Daddy's response. "I could just tackle you and take the g.d. key away," he mumbled. How are you supposed to deal with a man like this?

Now in the convalescent hospital, he watches Shirley MacLaine talk about the chakras on a video my sister brought in to help him relax and accept "life." Once in a while, he turns his head slowly toward me and stares at me with his almost lifeless eyes. I hope he knows who I am.

Shirley's talking about balancing your emotions by concentrating on your yellow chakra, I'm crying, a lady down the hall is loudly moaning and no one is paying any attention to her. "Feel your love to humanity," Shirley is saying.

They say the most significant event in a man's life is the death of his father. I can see all kinds of psychological justifications for this theory, but I can't get my mind around any of them. I feel confused. My conscious mind hasn't been much disturbed by the thought of losing my dad, but I find myself crying for no apparent reason, feeling depressed for no apparent reason, anxious for no apparent reason, and excited about the future for no apparent reason. (If he dies, does that mean I win?)

My father finally gave it up on July 24, my sister's birthday. She called me that morning and I said, "Happy Birthday." She thanked me and said, "Daddy's gone." We just sat in silence for a while. I said "Happy Birthday" again, and she laughed, and we started discussing what to do.

Our plan was for my two sisters and me to take his ashes up to Tacoma and scatter them on Puget Sound where we had put some of my mother's ashes. Then we planned to tour Tacoma, looking at our old family homes, schools, and haunts.

The three of us rented a car in Portland and I was elected to drive the 150-mile trip, not because of my driving skills, but because we all knew one sister was a reckless maniac, and the other always looked at the person she was talking to instead of the road ahead. We left around 8:00 a.m. and got home around 11:00 that night.

Once in Tacoma, we had to find an appropriate place to, as they say, scatter the ashes. The bay front had changed a lot since we were kids. There were gates and locks everywhere and most of the open spaces swarmed with people. We didn't want to just heave the ashes out from some beach and watch the waves carry them back to the shore, and we didn't want a crowd of people around watching us. And we needed a place where the water was deeper. We considered renting a boat, but then suddenly remembered the marina where our parents had kept their boat. It seemed like the perfect place.

We drove there and parked outside the automatic gate and walked in when a departing car opened it. Everything seemed to be locked up. We briefly considered throwing the package of ashes over a cyclone fence into the bay on the other side, but quickly gave up that plan when we realized that the slightest error in the throw would result in the ashes splattering on a wooden walkway. We laughed at the image and at what our parents would have thought of it. We felt their presence strongly and knew they would have enjoyed the ridiculous humor of our situation.

We finally located the perfect place: the end of a long walkway out into the channel where the water was deep and the tides were strong.

On our way back to the car to get the ashes, we discovered we were locked inside the marina. It was about 11:00 in the morning on a weekday, and no one was in sight. We were trapped. We waited awhile, hoping someone would drive up and open the gate. No one came. We couldn't easily climb over the fence because of the barbed wire on top, but we noticed that the fence ran down into the water and that it would be possible to climb along the inside of the fence out into the water, go around the end, and come back up on the other side. I managed to get on the other side, with only one wet leg, and retrieve the ashes. I don't remember how I handed the ashes to my sisters, but I do remember it wasn't easy.

When I got back inside the marina, we took the ashes out onto the long dock and prepared a ceremony. We hadn't given it much prior thought; I think we knew it would work out as it should. I had brought the remainder of our mother's ashes to put together with his.

Opening the box was not easy. It took all three of us, working at it with my pocket knife, probably five minutes to get it open. Inside we found a heavy clear plastic bag, weighing about five pounds. We cut an opening in it, poured our mother's ashes in, and talked about our lives with these two people. It was sunny and warm, and we felt sad and tearful, but very good about it all. We had been fortunate to have these parents. We had loved them and had been loved by them, and we felt that love strongly, as we sat on the dock, talking. We read aloud some things from some books, said our last words, and lowered the last of our parents into the waters of Puget Sound. We watched the ashes sink slowly down to about fifteen feet, where they disappeared from sight.

No one said anything. We sat and thought our own thoughts and looked out over the water for a long time. We finally said "Goodbye Mom and Dad. We love you," and walked back up the dock. Of course we were still locked in.

Back into real life. We burst into laughter. It was ludicrous. Here we had just performed this sacred, loving ceremony in honor of those who had given us life, and now we were unceremoniously trapped by some stupid mechanical device that was unimpressed with our spiritual glow.

Eventually a car came in and the smirking driver let us out. The rest of that day was incredibly fulfilling and enjoyable. We visited all of the old houses where we had lived, our old schools, and neighborhoods. We told each other stories about our experiences with our parents that had not been told before; we re-kindled our affection for each other. We even found a plaque at Daddy's college with his picture on it, showing that he was in their Athletic Hall of Fame.

The Eight-Week Syndrome

I've been shoeing horses for a lot of years and I think I'm beginning to learn some lessons about life from my customers. Horse owners come in all kinds of shapes and all kinds of attitudes and philosophies, and you can never really guess what they'll do. I've developed a respect for this. But, regardless of what they do or don't do, I've learned from them that life moves on. Especially in an eight-week cycle.

Let me explain. Typically, horses need to have their feet done every eight weeks. There are some bizarre exceptions to this, but generally the horseshoer shows up every eight weeks. My usual greeting to my customers has always been something like, "How's it going?" or "How have you been?" These are not rhetorical questions. A lot of horse owners, who trust the care of their horse to the shoer, also trust the shoer with the details of their lives. Horseshoers frequently take on the role of lay therapist, sometimes just being a good listener, sometimes offering advice, sometimes strongly recommending certain actions. I'm becoming more of a listener because I'm slowly learning that advice isn't really needed. Listening is.

A common response to my question about how they were doing has often been something negative: a sickness, a job loss, a breakup in a relationship—the usual concerns that people have. I always commiserated. Many of these troubles were quite disheartening and I took some of them home with me to worry about in my off time.

But when I came back in eight weeks, after my opening greeting of "How's your problem going?" almost without exception my customer would say something like, "Oh, everything's OK now," or "That never came about," or "I'm really glad I got fired because now I've got this great new job and I'm making twice as much money. I can't believe I was so worried." What I consistently find is that no matter what the problem had been eight weeks ago, it often was no longer a problem. The issue had been resolved, been fixed, or the customer had just moved beyond it. Sometimes a new problem had replaced the old one, but the lesson was that the old one was usually gone.

The regularity of this phenomenon makes me look more closely at my own life, and as a consequence, I find it more difficult to consider suicide, or the Foreign Legion as answers to my own problems—simply because I'm pretty certain they'll be gone in eight weeks. There's a good chance that something equally troublesome will have replaced them, but then I just have to wait another eight weeks and *that* one will be gone, too. And I find that I enjoy life a lot more knowing this.

Sometimes, these days, I worry that my customers will notice that I'm not as fully engaged in their problems as I used to be. I hope this doesn't cause any of them to switch to another therapist, but should I worry about that? If they fire me, I'm sure I'll have another, even better customer, in eight weeks.

This eight-week theory works pretty well on the smaller troubles we have in life, and sometimes on the bigger ones, too, like for example, the loss of a job or the break up of some relationship. Occasionally these also can reach some kind of resolution in eight weeks.

But sometimes it takes more than waiting eight weeks. I think about the deaths of my mother and father where eight weeks isn't going to fix anything. I'm aware that it's been a long time since I've seen them, and I miss them. When they were alive and living in another state, I often didn't visit them for an entire year. The longer I was away, the more I wanted to see them, and eventually I would go for a visit, fill up on family enough to hold me for another year, and leave. When I ran low on family contact, I'd return home again. But that doesn't work with death. I can return to the town of my youth, but that doesn't fill the void. Nothing does. Not even eight weeks.

I guess it's a matter of trying to see the big picture, a concept I'm not always eager to apply to my own life, although perfectly willing to foist off on other people.

I remember an incident with my dogs that got me to thinking about this theological perspective. I always took my dogs to work with me. They were chained in the back of my pickup so they wouldn't fall or jump out, and the usual procedure was that I would unchain them when we got to our horseshoeing destination and they would leap out and go about their activities.

One day, however, as I was about to unchain them at a new location, an old ranch hand casually remarked, "I wouldn't let them dogs out, was I you." When I asked why not, he said, "See those two dogs up by the house? If your dogs get out, them two will come down here and kill your dogs." I looked up and saw two big dogs calmly lying there watching us. I looked over at my dogs in the truck. They were jumping and whining, pulling at their chains as if to say, "Please, please, oh please! Let us out!" All they wanted in the world was to be let out. They couldn't see the Big Picture. They couldn't know that if I gave them their immediate wish, those two dogs would come down and kill them. The Big Picture.

I try to think about this when things aren't going the way I want them to, like with the death of my mother and my father. This Big Picture is harder for me to understand, but I'm beginning to discover that if I apply that eight-week theory I've learned from my customers to most of the "problems" that occur in my life, then I'm in a better position to understand and accept whatever the Big Picture has in store for me. I think that's because I'm not always running around all upset over the little irritations in my life, so I can be more objective and insightful about the bigger things. If I'm carrying a sack of petty little irritants around in my tool box, I'm in a good position to get myself in deeper trouble because I'm not paying attention to the horse I'm working on. And there's nothing like a broken leg or a bashed in head to get your attention.

I'm finding the eight week idea works well for me because the problems in my life are mostly insignificant. The freedom I gain from applying the eight-week syndrome theory to these little situations helps me to be stronger, more relaxed, and accepting of life. I feel better equipped to face whatever life brings me. I thank my customers and the horses for this, but my old horseshoeing buddy, Gary Belvin, said it best: "Ron, your problem is you think too much. Just get under more horses."